Exceptional Cars

Ferrari 857S

Porter Press International

Also published by Porter Press International

Ultimate Series

John Fitzpatrick Group C Porsches - The Definitive History
Works 956 Porsches - The Definitive History

Great Cars Series

No. 1 – Jaguar Lightweight E-type – The autobiography of 4 WPD
No. 2 – Porsche 917 – The autobiography of 917-023
No. 3 – Jaguar D-type – The autobiography of XKD 504
No. 4 – Ferrari 250GT SWB – The autobiography of 2119 GT
No. 5 – Maserati 250F – The autobiography of 2528
No. 6 – ERA – The autobiography of R4D
No. 7 – Ferrari 250GTO – The autobiography of 4153 GT
No. 8 – Jaguar Lightweight E-type – The autobiography of 49 FXN
No. 9 – Jaguar C-type – The autobiography of XKC 051
No. 10 – Lotus 18 – The autobiography of Stirling Moss's '912'
No. 11 – Ford GT40 – The autobiography of 1075
No. 12 – Alfa Romeo Monza – The autobiography of the celebrated 2211130
No. 13 – Bugatti Type 50 – The autobiography of Bugatti's first Le Mans car
No. 14 - Shelby Daytona Cobra Coupe - The autobiography of CSX2300

Exceptional Cars Series

No. 1 – Iso Bizzarrini – The remarkable history of A3/C 0222
No. 2 – Jaguar XK120 – The remarkable history of JWK 651
No. 3 – Ford GT40 MkII – The remarkable history of 1016
No. 4 – The First Three Shelby Cobras
No. 5 – Aston Martin Ulster – The remarkable history of CMC 614
No. 6 – Maserati 4CLT – The remarkable history of chassis no. 1600
No. 7 – Ferrari 250 LM – The remarkable history of 6313
No. 8 – Ferrari 250 GT SWB– The remarkable history of 2689

Porter Profiles

No. 1 – Austin Healey – The story of DD 300
No. 2 – Jaguar D-type – The story of XKD 526

Bespoke books

The Le Mans Model Collection 1949-2009 (three-book set)
Derek Bell - All my Porsche races
DB4 G.T. Continuation - History in the making
One Formula, 50 years of car design – Gordon Murray
The Self Preservation Society - 50 Years of The Italian Job

Scrapbooks

Stirling Moss Scrapbook 1929-1954
Stirling Moss Scrapbook 1955
Stirling Moss Scrapbook 1956-1960
Stirling Moss Scrapbook 1961
Graham Hill Scrapbook 1929-1966
Murray Walker Scrapbook
Martin Brundle Scrapbook
Barry Cryer Comedy Scrapbook
Mini Scrapbook

The Jaguar Portfolio

Ultimate E-type – The Competition Cars
Jaguar E-type – The Definitive History (2nd edition)
Original Jaguar XK (3rd edition)
Jaguar Design – A Story of Style
Saving Jaguar

Deluxe leather-bound, signed, limited editions with slipcases are available for many titles.
Books available from retailers or signed copies (of most titles) direct from the publishers.
To order simply phone +44 (0)1584 781588, visit the website or email sales@porterpress.co.uk
Keep up-to-date with news about current books and new releases at: www.porterpress.co.uk

Exceptional Cars

Ferrari 857S
The remarkable history of 0578M

Ian Wagstaff

Porter Press International

©Porter Press International Ltd

All rights reserved. No part of this publication may be reproduced, stored in a retrieval system or transmitted, in any form or by any means, electronic, mechanical, photocopying, recording or otherwise, without prior permission in writing from the publisher.

First published in April 2020

978-1-913089-08-5

Published by
Porter Press International Ltd

Hilltop Farm, Knighton-on-Teme, Tenbury Wells, WR15 8LY, UK
Tel: +44 (0)1584 781588
sales@porterpress.co.uk
www.porterpress.co.uk

Edited by Giles Chapman
Design & Layout by Adrian Morris
Creative Direction and Design of Gallery pages Joel Berg

Printed by Gomer Press Ltd

COPYRIGHT

We have made every effort to trace and acknowledge copyright holders and we apologise in advance for any unintentional omission. We would be pleased to insert the appropriate acknowledgement in any subsequent edition.

Contents

Introduction		7

Factory Days — 8

1	Reign of the four-cylinders	10
2	A year in Italy	20
3	The lanes of Ireland	32
4	Subdued in Sicily	44
5	Factory finale in America	52

In Private Hands — 68

6	The other side of the world	70
7	Viking saga	80

A Fitting Tribute — 90

8	Modern times	92
9	Photo gallery	100

Acknowledgements	124
Bibliography	125
Index	126

Introduction

Ferrari 857S chassis number 0578M completely encapsulates Italian road racing. Just once during its first season did it compete abroad and, granted, its first race was on the purpose-built circuit of Monza. It is, though, on the open highway, blasting through Sicilian villages or up spectator-lined mountain roads in the Valle d'Aosta region that one pictures the four-cylinder 0578M – an evocatively shaped two seater, appropriately red in hue.

This style of racing dated back to the first days of motor sport, held mainly over French routes but with the first Coppa Florio in 1900 on Italian roads. By 1955 the race was in its twilight years. Within two seasons, the Mille Miglia was run for the last time as an outright race. The Targa Florio staggered on into the early 1970s but motor racing was heading for confinement within soulless, purpose-built autodromes, where the heart would beat just a little less.

In some ways, 0578M also reflects this change. Within two years it had decamped to New Zealand, racing on the kind of airfield circuits that had sprung up since the Second World War and which would pave the way for the tracks of today.

The 1955 season was an inauspicious one for Ferrari. Its once stellar driver line-up had dwindled and, as far as Grand Prix racing was concerned, the glory days of 1952 and 1953 seemed a long way back. The team was also losing the grip it had held on the World Sportscar Championship since its inception in 1952. In a bid to halt the Mercedes-Benz racing juggernaut, Ferrari took simple, classically-designed four-cylinder sports cars that had hitherto competed with 2- and 3-litre engines, and installed 3.5-litre powerplants. Chassis 0578M was one of these. It was already a veteran of events in its native land but the change of engine propelled it on to the World Championship stage (although it did revert to 3-litre power for the Dundrod Tourist Trophy) and on to a second place in the following year's Buenos Aires 1,000km.

In 1977 the Mille Miglia was revived as a regularity event for the type of car that had participated in the 'real' race. The Ferrari factory did not use 0578M for the original Mille Miglia but it is fitting to report that its current custodian has shown his understanding of the car's pedigree by returning back to the hilly Italian countryside to take part in the modern equivalent.

Ian Wagstaff
Chinnor, England
February 2020

- Ferrari 857S 0578M has been faithfully restored and now appears as it was at the 1956 12-Hours of Sebring. It has also been able to return to its Italian road racing roots by participating in the modern recreation of the Mille Miglia.
Author

Part 1
Factory Days

It was all very different in the 1950s. Today, Ferrari, as a factory entrant, concentrates on just one series of events with a mere two cars per race. Admittedly, there will be modern Ferraris racing throughout the world in the GT category, but these will be privately entered. These days, for the Ferrari works team and their ardent followers, it is all about the narrow focus of the Formula One World Championship and so one could argue that motor racing has lost some of its allure.

During the 1950s, the factory spread its net far and wide. There was the then young Formula One World Championship, and on four occasions during the decade one of its drivers took the title. In addition, the *Scuderia*'s entries would turn up for non-championship Formula One events, of which there were then many, Formula Two, *Formule Libre* and a whole gamut of sports car events. The latter ranged from rounds of the World Sportscar Championship – launched in 1953 and won by Ferrari five times during the 1950s – to minor races and hillclimbs in which factory cars were often entered in several different engine capacity categories.

The four-cylinder-engined sports cars Ferrari developed during this period were raced both by the factory and by privateers. With their variety of capacities, they could be entered in both under- and over-2-litre classes, and their versatility shone in the spread of events they contested. Chassis 0578M was one of these. Its tale is complex but the car's use by the *Scuderia* during 1955 and early 1956 paints a picture of the life of a hard-working factory Ferrari sports car during the decade.

Looking just as it does now, 0578M competing at Sebring in 1956. The Florida airfield race had been a round of the World Sports Car Championship since the series inception in 1953.
The Revs Institute for Automotive Research/Tom Burnside

Chapter 1
Reign of the Four-Cylinders

The first car to race under the evocative Ferrari marque, the 125, was announced in the winter of 1946-47. Powering it was a Gioachino Colombo-designed V12 engine of 1,497cc. It set the scene where, when one thinks of Ferrari sports cars, one thinks multi-cylinder. 'Unquestionably, the most famous racing and high-performance GT engine of the post-Second World War era is the Ferrari V12,' wrote Hans Tanner in his seminal tome on the marque *Ferrari*.

However, there are exceptions to this picture. Ferrari built a 1,985cc in-line four-cylinder engine for Formula Two (F2) in the early 1950s. Although Enzo Ferrari's cars were then virtually unbeatable in this class, he had begun to notice that the opposition was becoming stiffer. Aurelio Lampredi had just been appointed chief engineer when it was decided to abandon the 12-cylinder engines then being used for F2. These lacked enough torque for the more complex circuits and Lampredi felt that a straightforward four-cylinder would compensate for this. By the spring of 1951 two versions were on the test bench, a 2-litre and a 2.5-litre, the latter making a first race appearance at Bari with Piero Taruffi at the wheel.

With the announcement that the Drivers' World Championship would be for 2-litre F2 cars during 1952 and 1953, Ferrari decided to go all-out with the dry-sump four-cylinder engine to power its Type 500 single-seater. The result was back-to-back championships for factory driver Alberto Ascari. With the return of Formula One and an engine capacity of 2.5-litre in 1954, Ferrari stuck to the four-cylinder configuration, although with far less success, until it took over Lancia's V8 engines for the 1956 F1 season.

It was a different matter with sports cars. Enzo Ferrari's first car, although it did not bear his name, was the pre-Second World War Auto Avio Costruzioni Type 815, and it used an eight-cylinder power unit. Then came the first V12 in the squat Ferrari 125. During the Second World War, Enzo Ferrari had been planning for a racing future, with his schemes based on a single design of V12 engine. Maserati was using four, Talbot six and Alfa Romeo eight so, as Tanner asked, why not 12? This remained the case for a number of years but, perhaps inevitably following the success in F2, the experience gained with four-cylinders would be transferred to the sports cars. While continuing to develop and use the V12s, Ferrari tried out the four-cylinder in a sports-racing car for the first time in the spring of 1953. Two cars made their debut in the Gran Premio dell'Autodromo at Monza that June. Mike Hawthorn finished fourth in the 250MM-based, 2.5-litre 625TF, while Alberto Ascari led the race in the bored-out 2.9-litre 735S, before colliding with another competitor. Umberto Magioli, who features strongly later in this story, then took the 735S to the Senigallia Grand Prix a couple of months later where, after showing a display of speed in front of Enzo Ferrari (making one of his very rare post-war appearances at a race), he retired with a broken connecting-rod.

The 2.5-litre test programme was now brought to an end and it was not until that December that another four-cylinder Ferrari sports car appeared at a racetrack. Ascari had just won his second World Championship with the 2-litre four-cylinder motor, so perhaps it is not surprising that this size unit was installed in the new 500 Mondial that made its debut at the Casablanca 12-hours,

Alberto Ascari and the four-cylinder Ferrari 500 Formula 2 car dominated the Drivers' World Championship in 1952 and 1953.
LAT Images

Reign of the Four-Cylinders

Think Ferrari and one is likely to think of multi-cylinder engines. The initial car to carry the famed name, the 125 was powered by a Colombo-designed V12. Enzo Ferrari (centre) examines the new creation.
The Revs Institute for Automotive Research/Rodolfo Mailander

● Umberto Maglioli finished third overall, driving an in-line, four-cylinder Ferrari 735S Barchetta, on the 1953 Copa d'Oro dell Dolomiti.
The Revs Institute for Automotive Research

where it was placed second. It is said the Mondial name reflected Ascari's world titles and it was the legendary Italian who, along with Luigi Villoresi, drove the car on this occasion. The pair also finished first in class. The first batch of customer 500 Mondials was delivered the following April.

Ferrari was working on a new 3-litre four-cylinder car at the same time as finalising the smaller 500 Mondial.

It used the Tipo 555 engine as a basis. This development of Lampredi's design saw the bore increased from the 90mm of the previous year to 103mm, while the stroke remained at 90mm. The capacity was now 2,999.62cc, brake-horsepower was 260, and maximum revs 6,400. It was designated the Tipo 119, as opposed to the Tipo 111 used in the 500 Mondial. Use was now being made of a pair of Weber 58DCOA/3 carburettors. This car which,

Reign of the Four-Cylinders

● The smooth lines of the four-cylinder Ferrari 750 Monza are seen here in 1955 at the track after which it was named. *Cesare Martinengo*

like the 500 Mondial, featured a Tipo 510 chassis, was known as the 750 Monza and it is here that the story of chassis 0578M properly begins. When it first appeared at Monza in 1955, 0578M was known as a 750 Monza but it was visually different from the cars of 1954.

The four-cylinder cars had been used in the 1954 World Championship alongside the V12s, as the *Scuderia* fought to beat Lancia to the title. Vittorio Marzotto finished second on the Mille Miglia in a 500 Mondial which contemporary author Cyril Posthumus observed was '…of obvious Grand Prix derivation'. At Dundrod for the Tourist Trophy, Ferrari brought along a pair of 750 Monzas as opposed to the more unwieldy V12s because the larger cars were less suited to the lanes of Ireland. Indeed, it was reported that the 750 Monza of Mike Hawthorn and Maurice Trintignant seemed ideal for the

Ferrari 857S | 13

Reign of the Four-Cylinders

Cyril Posthumus wrote that in the 1954 Mille Miglia was 'Vittorio Marzotto's new 2-litre four-cylinder Ferrari of obvious Grand Prix derivation, called the Mondial.' With the demise of the larger Ferraris, Marzotto was to finish second to Alberto Ascari's Lancia.
The Revs Institute for Automotive Research/Rodolfo Mailander

course, and led on the road from the second lap. Aided by Ferrari pit-work that was far superior to that of Lancia, the pair sped on to an emphatic win. Except, it was not actually a win. For the last time, the TT was decided on handicap and, with the smallest class given a 155-mile start over the 3-litre cars, it proved impossible for even the hard-charging Hawthorn to catch the tiny victorious DB-Panhard of Paul Armagnac and Gérard Laurea. As far as the World Championship was concerned, that did not matter; points were awarded on road positions, enabling Ferrari to extend its lead on Lancia. There were no factory Ferraris for the final race of the series, the Carrera Panamericana, and it was back to the brutish 375s now in private hands to clinch the title for the marque. Nevertheless, the four-cylinder cars, with their second and 'first' places in Italy and Ireland, had played their part in retaining the championship for Ferrari. In the following season, Mercedes-Benz would unleash

Reign of the Four-Cylinders

its formidable 300SLR, so Ferrari would have to up its game. What happened to 0578M that year to combat the German challenge is part of the story.

Lampredi had left Ferrari for Fiat, a move that arguably heralded the end for the four-cylinder engines. Vittorio Bellantani, Alberto Massimino – a chassis and suspension expert recruited from Maserati – and the young Andrea Frachetti took over his work, while Luigi Bazzi remained as development engineer. Also into the mix came legendary racing car designer Vittorio Jano, who persuaded Ferrari to return to 12 cylinders. However, in 1955 the four-cylinder was to be developed further to last a couple more seasons.

In its final configuration the engine had a capacity of 3,431cc, and was known internally as the Tipo 129. It was installed in a multi-tubular Tipo 510 chassis evolved from those in the 750 Monza and 500 Mondial. These Tipo 510 *evoluzione* had first appeared just days before the Supercortemaggiore Grand Prix at Monza in May 1955, one of them being 0578M. They featured a fundamentally redesigned version of the Scaglietti body with higher flanks *fianchi alti*, the side skirts stopping above the level of the chassis side members to boost ventilation; the side vents were enlarged for the same reason. Ferrari historian Antoine Prunet declared this new, less bulky bodywork was 'more pleasant' to view from the left side because it was well filled by the exhaust pipes, while the right side was bare and exposed.

Massimino's influence could be seen in the changes made to the Tipo 510 chassis itself. Its behaviour had been criticised because of the polar moment of inertia generated by the chassis's very short wheelbase. To achieve better weight distribution, various repositionings of the engine were carried out with a front cross-member that created a V-shaped angle instead of the previous rectangular box. Less obvious was the fact that the rear part of the chassis had been made more rigid using extra tubes. The wheelbase was lengthened by 80mm, something that was made noticeable externally by welds on the main side rails, particularly at the level of the gearlever.

While nine cars were fitted with the new, high-sided bodywork, it seems that only six had the chassis

Aurelio Lampredi

● Aurelio Lampredi (seen here, right, with Alberto Ascari) brought about a change at Ferrari with his four-cylinder engine design.
Grand Prix Library

Former aero engine designer Aurelio Lampredi was employed by Ferrari as assistant to the famed Gioacchino Colombo, designer of the Alfa Romeo 158/159 cars that took the first two World Championships, as well as the V12 engine that is an absolute touchstone of the Ferrari marque. He joined Ferrari shortly after the Second World War, then left briefly to return to his pre-war employer Isotta Fraschini after falling out with Giuseppe Busso who was in charge of the Ferrari technical office. However, Busso himself departed Ferrari late in 1947 and Lampredi was soon back.

He was closely involved in the development of the V12 engine, convinced that a naturally-aspirated engine could challenge the might of the supercharged Alfa Romeos. This theory went strongly against pre-war design trends, yet the 'long-block' V12 helped forge Ferrari's wonderful reputation. When Colombo left in 1949 Lampredi, who was then just into his thirties, was promoted to chief engineer at the *Scuderia*.

He would soon bring about a dramatic change in course for Ferrari, opting to abandon the V12s for Formula Two and design a four-cylinder engine, the Tipo 500. Better torque at low speeds, significant weight reduction, and fewer moving parts were all felt to be benefits over the V12. The result was that, when the World Championship moved to F2 for the 1952 and 1953 seasons, Ferrari dominated the series. Engines of two, three and 3.5-litre, developments of this power unit, were also used in 0578M.

When Ferrari took over Lancia's racing programme in 1956, the latter's V8 engine designed by Vittorio Jano became its weapon of choice, and Lampredi's work for the *Scuderia* was effectively over. That year Lampredi elected to join Fiat where he eventually became Director of Motor-Vehicle Planning, and oversaw the company's engine development strategy for the next 22 years. He then returned to his sporting roots when he became Technical Director at Abarth in 1972, helping the team to win three World Rally Championships with the Fiat Abarth 131.

Sergio Scaglietti

On the death of his father the teenage Sergio Scaglietti found work in a garage near Maranello, repairing the bodywork of cars that had been damaged in accidents. This brought him to the attention of locally-based Enzo Ferrari, who initially kept him busy repairing customers' crashed racing cars. Scaglietti then upped his game and opened his own coachbuilding firm, Carrozzeria Scaglietti, in 1951. When Ferrari then examined the superb quality of a new body he made for a client's Touring Barchetta, he invited Scaglietti to work directly for the factory on brand new designs.

The four-cylinder cars were among the first he was involved with. The race debut of the 750 Monza in 1954 saw a pair of cars entered, the winner driven by Mike Hawthorn and Umberto Maglioli, and the second-placed by José Froilán González and Maurice Trintignant. The former featured a Scaglietti-designed and built two-seater body. This was similar to the one seen on the Type 735S raced at Monza and Senigallia the previous year, designed by Aurelio Lampredi and built by the Autodromo coachwork company in Modena. The latter used bodywork designed by Enzo's son Dino and made by Scaglietti, and was subsequently used for all production 750 Monzas. Despite its origins, the new 3.5-litre 857S used fundamentally new bodywork, a reworking of the Scaglietti body by Pinin Farina that was also built by Carrozzeria Scaglietti.

Scaglietti tended to design his shapes by eye, rarely drawing them out in advance but instead shaping them directly over the chassis, and relying on traditional metal-bashing skills.

● Sergio Scaglietti tended to design his shapes by eye. *Newspress*

modifications, and can therefore be described as true Tipo 510 *evoluzione*. Chassis 0578M, which had first appeared at Monza earlier in the year with a 3-litre engine, was one such.

These cars used a variety of the four-cylinder power units, swapping between the 2-litre Tipo 111 and the 3-litre 119 during the early months of their life. The engine choice all depended upon the nature of the race ahead, some of which had a 2-litre ceiling for entries. It was only at September's Dundrod Tourist Trophy – with Ferrari needing to upgrade to combat Mercedes-Benz – that 0578 was fitted with a new 3.5-litre engine, although in the end this was not used in the race. For its last two races as a factory car, it had just such a unit and so can be called an 857S, referring to is capacity per cylinder of 857.93cc. That said, it seems this designation was not used until later to distinguish it from the 860 Monza, which was the ultimate incarnation of the four-cylinder cars. For its time 'down under' in 1956 and 1957, 0578M reverted to a 3-litre engine, and so was again known as a 750 Monza. It was, though, with the 3.5-litre engine that it really made its mark, Therefore, it is fitting that today it is so-powered and can be remembered as an 857S, a more appropriate reflection of its factory heritage.

The Tipo 129 differed from the Tipo 111 and Tipo 119 engines in that its 102x105mm dimensions gave it a greater stroke than its bore, a configuration that Prunet points out was unique in Ferrari history. A total of 310bhp was eventually claimed, a decided improvement on the smaller four-cylinders. The longer stroke made the engine slightly higher than the two smaller four-cylinder units. This meant bulges had to be made in the bonnet, added at first to accommodate an experimental forward positioning of the engine.

It appears that four of the *evoluzione* cars were actually raced by the factory: 0578 itself; 0584, with which it would later be confused; 0570; and 0588. It is possible that 0568 was also used on one occasion. Prunet points out that the term *evoluzione* never featured on official documents but can be supported 'on the strength of unofficial verbal definition circulating at Maranello'.

Reign of the Four-Cylinders

The weakness of both the four- and six-cylinder Ferraris had become apparent under the weight of pressure from Mercedes-Benz across more than one discipline. Both the World Drivers and Sportscar championships had gone to Germany for 1955. Italy, which had hitherto enjoyed dominance, was not impressed and the competition department of Lancia – closed down during the year – was handed over to Ferrari. The Formula One team was the immediate beneficiary but soon advantages began to be seen for the sports cars too. Twelve-cylinder engines returned but the four-cylinders still had life in them. As far as the works cars were concerned, the last hurrah was the 860 Monza, a machine little changed from the 857S although a new front coil spring suspension improved handling and made it more competitive. Peter Collins, partnered by intrepid photographer Louis Klemantaski, finished second on the 1956 Mille Miglia behind a V12 290MM, with Luigi Musso third in another 860 Monza. Juan Manuel Fangio, now a Ferrari man, albeit not for long, and Eugenio Castellotti followed this up with another second in the Nürburgring 1,000km, having been fastest in practice. The final round of that year's championship, the Swedish Grand Prix was one of those confusing endurance events where factory drivers swapped between cars apparently indiscriminately. Two of the big 290MMs completed the full distance but one lap behind in third was an 860 Monza driven by Hawthorn, Alfonso de Portago, Peter Collins and Duncan Hamilton; the last named had recently been sacked by Jaguar for disobeying team orders. Fourth, and first in its class, was a locally-entered 750 Monza driven by John Kvanström, who will feature again in this tale, and Erik Lundgren.

Ferrari was back on top of the World Championship, having won four of the five rounds. The four-cylinders had had their moments but even the most successful had been beaten by at least one of the V12s, so they did not contribute to Ferrari's score. The only four-cylinder Ferraris that turned up for the first round of the following season were locally-entered back markers. The four-cylinders' frontline days were over.

- (Above) Twelve cylinder engines were still Ferrari's front line attack in 1954. Umberto Maglioli crashed this 375 Plus on the Mille Miglia having been lying in second place.
  The Revs Institute for Automotive Research/ Rodolfo Mailander

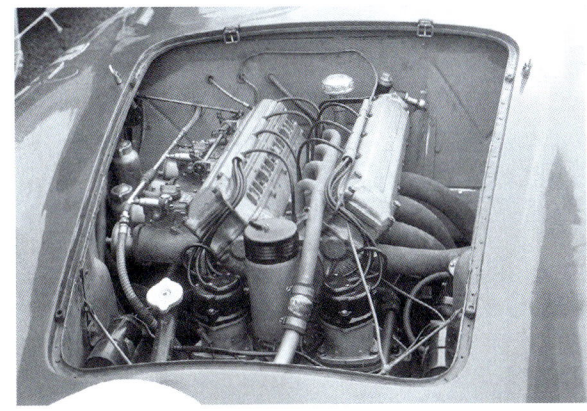

- (Left) An in-line four-cylinder engine is perhaps not what one expects to find in a Ferrari sportscar but it was this that powered the 857S.
  The Klemantaski Collection/Louis Klemantaski

Reign of the Four-Cylinders

- The four-cylinder Ferraris that went to New Zealand at the start of 1957, to be raced by Ken Wharton and Ross Jensen, were, at the time, fitted with three-litre engines.
Terry Marshall Archives

- (Below) The two-litre 500 Mondial was the smallest of the four-cylinder Ferrari sportscars. Here Franco Cortese's example races on to 14th place in the 1954 Mille Miglia.
The Revs Digital Library/ Rodolfo Mallander

Reign of the Four-Cylinders

(Above) The Ferrari 860 Monza of Juan Manuel Fangio and Eugenio Castellotti in the Karussell during the 1956 Nürburgring 1,000km.
The Revs Digital Library/ George Phillips

(Left) Alfonso de Portago finished third driving a four-cylinder Ferrari 857S in the 1957 Cuban Grand Prix, which took place on a street circuit in Havana. His girlfriend of the time, actress Linda Christian, joined him at the start.
The Revs Digital Library/Tom Burnside

Chapter 2
A Year in Italy

There can be no better place for a new Italian competition car to make its debut than the Parco di Monza. The very surroundings and atmosphere exude the country's motor racing heritage. The factory's redesigned 750 Monzas made their initial race appearance here on 29 May 1955, three days after having first been seen in public.

29 May 1955, Grand Prix Supercortemaggiore, Monza *Car number 16, Mike Hawthorn/Umberto Maglioli:* **finished 2nd.**
Newly-built chassis 0578M was entered for the Supercortemaggiore to be driven by Mike Hawthorn and Umberto Maglioli. The young Englishman was no longer a Ferrari factory driver. He had left the team to join Vanwall for Formula One, and Jaguar for sports car events. However, Jaguar did allow him to be a late nominee for his previous employer at Monza and, for Mike, it was a great homecoming because he was reunited with his friend Umberto. However, whatever pleasure he had from this was overshadowed when, just after lunchtime on the Thursday before the race, he arrived at Monza and wandered into the bar to be told – as he recalled in his autobiography, *Challenge Me The Race* – by a shocked chief mechanic Meazza: "*Ascari e morto*."

As far as Hawthorn was aware, the great Italian had been none the worse for crashing his Lancia into the harbour at Monaco a few days before. But then, just an hour before Mike's arrival at Monza, Alberto was killed in a Ferrari 750 Monza, the same car Hawthorn was scheduled to drive that weekend.

Like Hawthorn, Ascari was no longer a member of the Ferrari team, having departed for Lancia for the 1954 season with two World Championships already under his belt. Nonetheless, he turned up at Monza and asked Eugenio Castellotti if he could take his car out for a few trial laps of the circuit. Wearing a suit, and without his familiar blue helmet, he was obviously unprepared. Castellotti agreed, but within a couple of laps Ascari had crashed and been thrown fatally from the car. Hawthorn was of the opinion that inappropriate tyres were being used. 'The tyres we wanted to use for these cars were 6.50-16s, but they were not available at the time in the particular make we were using, and so 7.00-16 covers had to be fitted,' he wrote. 'I had driven the car with these tyres on it and found it very nasty indeed when it came to the Vialone Curve, where there were a lot of little ripples in the road surface. I came to the conclusion that the rims were too narrow for these tyres and I had them taken off my car.'

Italy was in mourning. But the race went ahead with an entry of 36 mainly Italian cars, limited to 3-litres. Following a minute's silence for Ascari and a rolling start, what Hawthorn described as a 'tremendous struggle' ensued as he and Maglioli battled against Jean Behra and Luigi Musso in their 3-litre Maserati. *Autocourse*, then a magazine rather than an annual publication, wondered why it was necessary to use two drivers per car for a race that lasted less than two hours. Such were attitudes in those days.

Initially, Hawthorn took the lead in 0578M ahead of the tenacious Behra. He calculated that he would be passed by the Maserati on the back of the circuit, but

The bonnet bulges signifying a larger engine would not appear on 0578M until the 1955 Tourist Trophy. Earlier in the year, at the Monza race, when it made its maiden appearance, the car still sported the smooth appearance of a conventional 750 Monza.
The Klemantaski Collection/JJF Archive

A Year in Italy

(Above) Hawthorn drove 0578M at Monza having just learnt of the death there of his former Ferrari team leader Alberto Ascari.
(Current owner's archive)

(Left) Driven by Mike Hawthorn, 0578M led at the start in its very first race, the 1955 Grand Prix Supercortemaggiore, eventually finishing second to Jean Behra's Maserati.
(Current owner's archive)

could get back in front coming out of the South Curve just before the start/finish line. That certainly suited him, as there was prize money for the leader of every lap. Mike wrote that Jean: '… obviously was not pleased about it and dropped back for a time, working out another strategy.'

When Hawthorn handed over to Maglioli, Behra took the lead, putting on extra speed to break José Froilán González's old sports car lap record, before handing over to Musso. As soon as the regulations allowed, Jean was back in the car, building up the lead to about a minute, which was reduced to 50 seconds when Hawthorn retook the wheel of 0578M. However, Hawthorn later confessed that he could not, at that point, see any chance of catching the Frenchman before the end. There was just one last hope that 0578M could score a maiden victory. 'Three laps before the end,' wrote Hawthorn, 'I could see the crowd frantically waving me on and I spotted Behra disappearing into the distance. He had run out of petrol just before the last corner and had managed to coast into the pits, where they tossed some fuel into the tank and sent him on his way with a mere 20 seconds' lead.'

Undisciplined spectators were already crowding on to the circuit, while the incompetent police guards started pushing around all the wrong people. Hawthorn 'pulled out all the stops' but was only able to cut Behra's lead down to 17sec. Still, for Mike it was a finish, something which, at that stage of his career, he rarely experienced.

5 June 1955, Circuito del Mugello
Car number 130, Umberto Maglioli: **finished 1st.**
One of the famed Italian road races, the Circuito del Mugello had lain dormant for 25 years. But it was a big part of the nation's motor racing backstory; back in 1920 Enzo Ferrari, then himself merely a racing driver, had taken

Umberto Maglioli, who was to become a regular driver of 0578M, is seen at the start of the 1955 Circuito del Mugello alongside OSCA driver Giulio Cabianca (86).
(Current owner's archive)

Ferrari 857S

A Year in Italy

● Umberto Maglioli took 0578M to victory on just its second outing, the Circuito del Mugello, having fought off Giulio Cabianca. *Current owner's archives*

second place in the race for Alfa Romeo. The race was revived on 5 June 1955 as an event for four capacity classes of sports car. The circuit, near Florence, was an absolute classic: 19.3km long, winding, and difficult. It was the scene of 0578M's first overall victory. Given that second place went to a slight 1.5-litre car, the OSCA of Giulio Cabianca, it seems as though Magliolo's task had been easy. Not so. Such was the nature of the course that Cabianca was briefly able to pass Umberto before having to yield to the superior power of the Ferrari. Nevertheless, the remarkable OSCA stayed ahead of the 2-litre factory Maseratis and the eventual third-place finisher, Dalla Favera in a 2-litre Ferrari. Magliolo also took the fastest lap, with a speed of 109.24kph, with Cabianca close behind with a second best 108.39kph. Chassis 0578M would score two more overall firsts but its finest result was yet to come.

19 June 1955, Coppa Shell, Imola
Car number 58, Umberto Magliolo: **finished 2nd.**
On 19 June 0578M was back at a purpose-built track, this time Imola and the 50-lap Coppa Shell, which was a key round of the Championship of Italy. The horrific tragedy of Le Mans (more later) had occurred the previous weekend and a number of stringent safety

precautions were hastily put in place. No passing was permitted 'at corners' or in front of the pits. Clear indication of pit stops had to be made at least 180m before a white line denoting the pits area. The contest was limited to cars of 2-litre and less, and run in an anticlockwise direction. Chassis 0578M was therefore fitted with the smaller power unit like a 500 Mondial. Magliolo was unable to repeat his Mugello performance, finishing second over 21sec behind Cesare Perdisa (Maserati A6GCS) who set a record average speed of 141.497kph. The leader for the initial 14 laps had been Luigi Bellucci before engine trouble caused his Ferrari to retire. That left Perdisa to forge ahead, followed by the Ferraris of Magliolo and Harry Schell, this order remaining unchanged right to the end. *Autocourse* was less than impressed by these two, stating they 'appeared to resign themselves to passive roles, instead of attempting to counteract the fervid driving of both Perdisa and Belluci.' Magliolo, it was reported, failed to launch a spirited attack on the eventual winner until it was far too late, although the journal did wonder if the *Scuderia* Ferrari pit control was at fault. 'The event was notable for the excellent shows put on by the relatively unknown and the mediocre performance of the more famous,' said a forthright *Autocourse*.

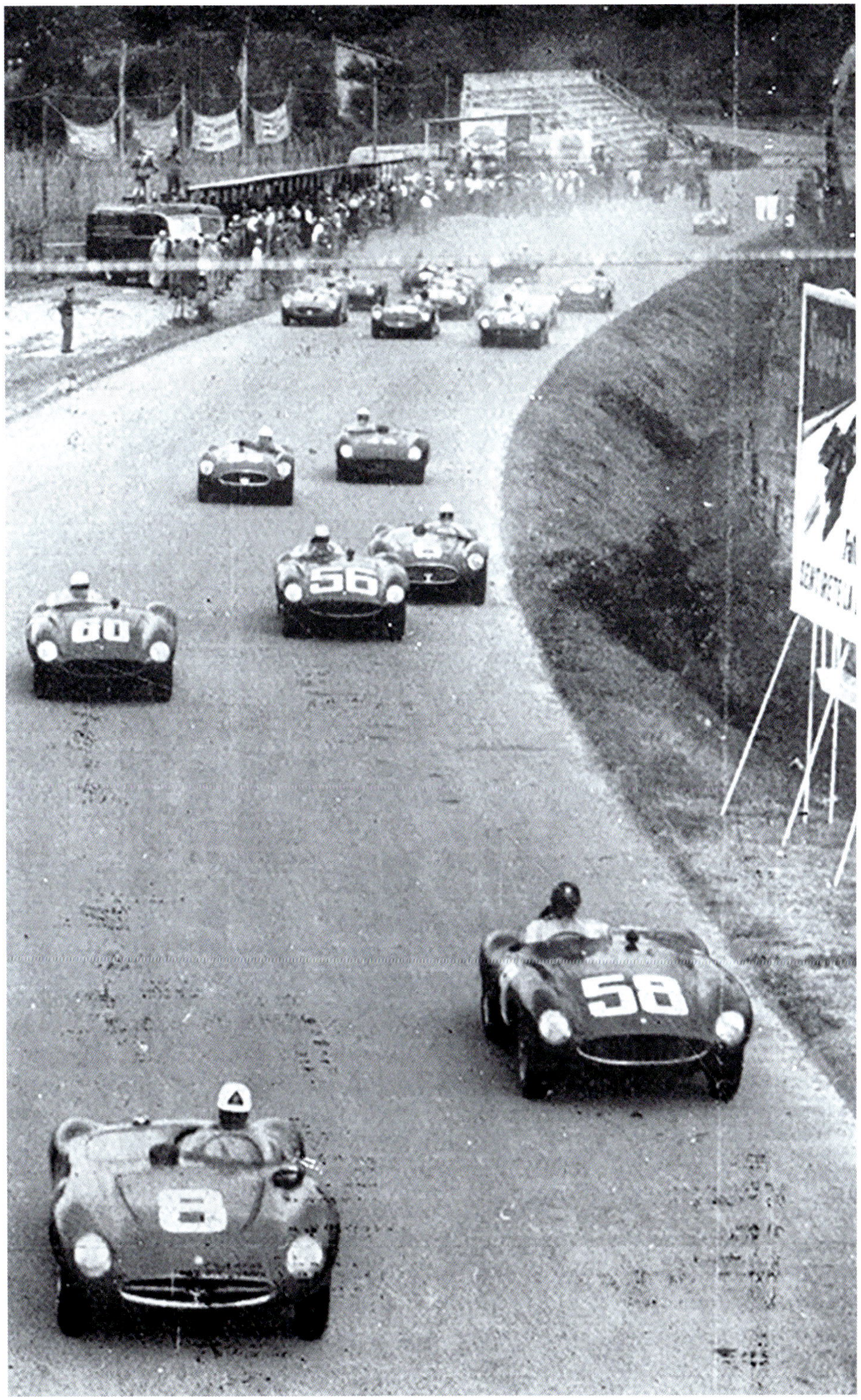

Luigi Bellucci's Maserati A6GCS (8) leads 0578M, driven by Umberto Maglioli (58) at Imola. Following them are Harry Schell (Ferrari), Piero Taruffi (Ferrari) and Cesare Perdisa (Maserati).
Adolfo Orsi

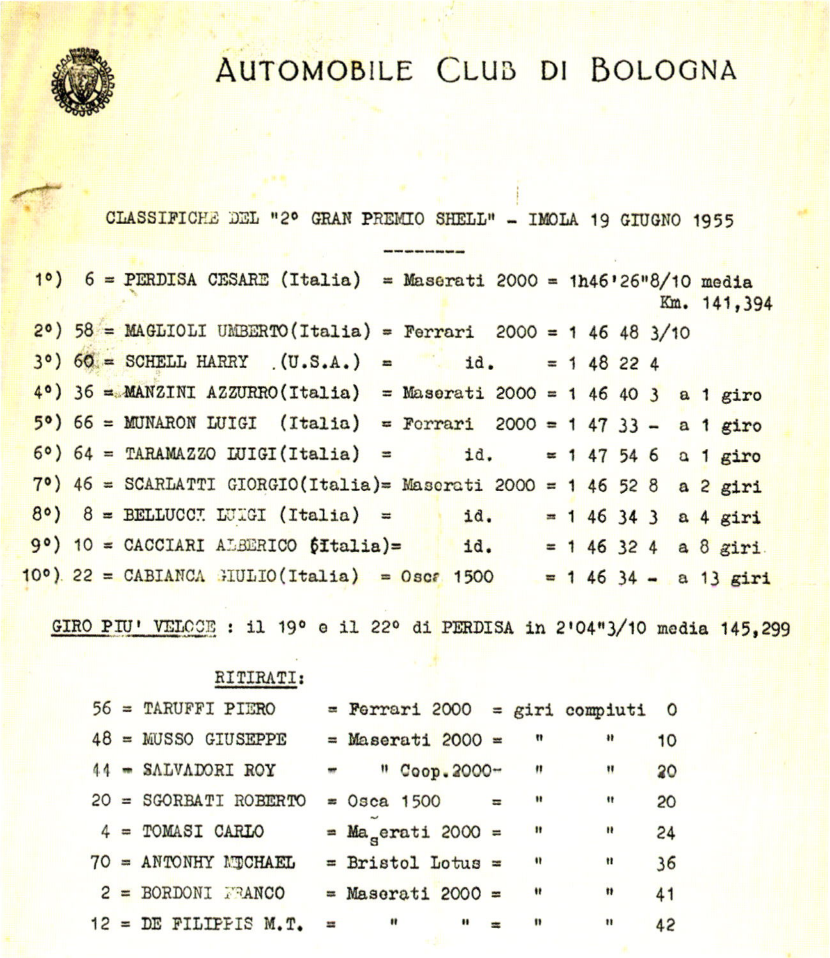

AUTOMOBILE CLUB DI BOLOGNA

CLASSIFICHE DEL "2° GRAN PREMIO SHELL" - IMOLA 19 GIUGNO 1955

1°)	6 = PERDISA CESARE (Italia)	= Maserati 2000	= 1h46'26"8/10 media Km. 141,394		
2°)	58 = MAGLIOLI UMBERTO(Italia)	= Ferrari 2000	= 1 46 48 3/10		
3°)	60 = SCHELL HARRY .(U.S.A.)	= id.	= 1 48 22 4		
4°)	36 = MANZINI AZZURRO(Italia)	= Maserati 2000	= 1 46 40 3	a 1 giro	
5°)	66 = MUNARON LUIGI (Italia)	= Ferrari 2000	= 1 47 33 -	a 1 giro	
6°)	64 = TARAMAZZO LUIGI(Italia)	= id.	= 1 47 54 6	a 1 giro	
7°)	46 = SCARLATTI GIORGIO(Italia)	= Maserati 2000	= 1 46 52 8	a 2 giri	
8°)	8 = BELLUCCI LUIGI (Italia)	= id.	= 1 46 34 3	a 4 giri	
9°)	10 = CACCIARI ALBERICO (Italia)	= id.	= 1 46 32 4	a 8 giri	
10°)	22 = CABIANCA GIULIO(Italia)	= Osca 1500	= 1 46 34 -	a 13 giri	

GIRO PIU' VELOCE : il 19° e il 22° di PERDISA in 2'04"3/10 media 145,299

RITIRATI:

56 = TARUFFI PIERO	= Ferrari 2000	= giri compiuti		0
48 = MUSSO GIUSEPPE	= Maserati 2000	= "	"	10
44 = SALVADORI ROY	= " Coop.2000	= "	"	20
20 = SGORBATI ROBERTO	= Osca 1500	= "	"	20
4 = TOMASI CARLO	= Maserati 2000	= "	"	24
70 = ANTONHY MICHAEL	= Bristol Lotus	= "	"	36
2 = BORDONI FRANCO	= Maserati 2000	= "	"	41
12 = DE FILIPPIS M.T.	= " "	= "	"	42

The results sheet for the Coppa, or Gran Premio, Shell, issued by the Automobile Club di Bologna, records Maglioli's second place with 0578M.
Adolfo Orsi

Mike Hawthorn

Two future Formula One World Champions were to race 0578M, both taking second place with the car. However, while Phil Hill drove it in the front rank Buenos Aires 1,000km, Mike Hawthorn's appearance with it was in a more modest event, albeit the car's debut, the 1955 Supercortemaggiore Grand Prix.

The first Englishman to win the sport's ultimate title, the effervescent Hawthorn's performances could range from mercurial to lacklustre. Races such as the 1953 French Grand Prix, where he outfoxed Juan Manuel Fangio after a side-by-side nailbiter, showed that, as Stirling Moss observed: 'He was the greatest fighter of them all.' Mike, though, suffered from a potentially life-shortening congenital defect of the kidneys, which at times left him feeling particularly low. It probably contributed to his inconsistent racing performances.

Like Hill, Hawthorn won just three World Championship Grands Prix but his victories at Reims (1953) and Penya Rhin (1954) were out of the top drawer. The Spanish race made him only the third Englishman after Henry Segrave and the enigmatic 'W. Grover-Williams' to win two GPs. Back in Reims in 1958, he led the French GP almost from start to finish. It was his sole GP win of the year while Stirling Moss had taken four, but the scoring system was with Hawthorn and he secured the World title by just one point.

Mike had three stints as a member of *Scuderia Ferrari*. The first came after his giant-killing performances in a Formula Two Cooper-Bristol. In theory, he left the Ferrari team for the start of the 1955 season to drive for Vanwall in Formula One and Jaguar in sports car racing. Thus, he was 'guesting' for his old team with Jaguar's permission when he made his sole appearance in 0578M. Feeling that the Vanwall still needed much development, he was back with Ferrari for the final three World Championship races of the year, while continuing with Jaguar for endurance events.

That the 'engaging' (Fangio's words) Hawthorn was also a fine sports car driver can be seen in his victories in the 1953 Spa 24-hours (with Nino Farina), the 1955 Sebring 12-hours (with Phil Walters), and Le Mans 24-hours (with Ivor Bueb), as well as the fact that, with Maurice Trintignant, he finished first on the road in the handicap-run Tourist Trophy of 1954. Both the Spa and TT results were achieved with Ferrari. At Le Mans in the Jaguar D-type, Mike had engaged in a furious battle for the lead with Fangio's Mercedes-Benz 300SLR. He was all the more determined because he passionately hated everything German. The ultimate withdrawal of the factory Mercedes following the infamous catastrophe on the pit straight left Hawthorn and Bueb to drive on to a sombre victory. Some have blamed Mike's action in slowing down for his pitstop for Pierre Levegh's horrific crash. With over 80 spectators killed, it was a heavy burden for the young Englishman to bear, although history has largely exonerated him from responsibility.

In January 1959, not long after he secured the World title by finishing second in Casablanca, Mike lost control of his much-modified Jaguar 3.4-litre saloon and crashed fatally just south of Guildford, Surrey. The rain was pouring down at the time and he had just come upon, and passed, the Mercedes-Benz 300SL of noted Formula One entrant Rob Walker. His biographer Chris Nixon was to muse on Hawthorn's need, once again, to beat anything German. Indeed, Mike referred to his Jaguar as 'the Merc-eater'. Walker eased off, later recalling his thought that 'this is all very well for a World Champion, but for me it's a bit too much.' However, for Mike Hawthorn, who had retired from motor racing immediately following his title victory, it was too late.

● In the 1950s and 1960s racing drivers tended to be more versatile than they are now. Mike Hawthorn was one of 0578M's two pilots to win both the World Championship and the Le Mans 24-hours.
Grand Prix Library/ Graham Gauld

3 July 1955, Bolzano-Mendola hillclimb
Eugenio Castellotti: **finished 1st.**

The talented but wild Eugenio Castellotti took over the wheel of 0578M – still with a 2-litre engine – for the 25km Bolzano-Mendola hillclimb on 3 July. The mountains were then an important part of the motor sport mix, although the first post-war European Hillclimb Championship was still two years away. In Britain, where the hills were mere sprint affairs, single-seaters dominated the scene, but on the Continent where the contests were over much longer distances the sports cars formed the main contenders.

A second overall victory was the end result for 0578M, with Castellotti repeating his victory there the previous year in a Lancia D24. A single Maserati A6GCS driven by Piero and Gino Valenzano was placed second and third respectively, with that man Giulio Cabianca fourth in his little OSCA.

The South Tyrolean hill, which rose 965m, was first tackled in 1930 and would continue to be used most years up until 1988, sometimes as a round of the European Championship.

10 July 1955, Coppa D'Oro Delle Dolomiti
Car number 138, Eugenio Castellotti: **finished 6th.**

It was back to circuit racing on the open roads for 0578M, although the car retained its 2-litre engine for the ninth Coppa D'Oro Delle Dolomiti. The event utilised the arduous 188-mile Cortina d'Ampezzo circuit and was often described as a kind of mountain Mille Miglia.

It was a peculiarity of this contest that the actual trophy went to the driver achieving the best aggregate time over three years, rather in the manner of the early Le Mans 24-hour races. Following his tiger-like performance at Mugello, it was fitting that this honour should fall to Cabianca and his plucky OSCA. As for the 1955 race, he finished third overall but still shook the more powerful opposition, beating it, according to *Autocourse* 'by a large margin' over the Falzarego, Pordoi and Castrozza sections. First home on the day was Olivier Gendebien, a future driver of 0578M. It was said this was 'remarkable proof' of his ability to learn an open road circuit, meaning the Belgian was able to beat so many experienced locals. However, it was also pointed out his Mercedes-Benz 300SL did enjoy a litre more capacity than the Italian cars.

But what of 0578M? Castellotti was again driving the car and was well in the lead when his team manager noted he was heading the International Category by a full 10 minutes. Out came the 'go slow' signal to which Eugenio complied. What the Ferrari pit had not noticed was that Gendebien's Mercedes-Benz was actually running in the Gran Turismo category, and was much closer to the race leader than 10 minutes! As a result, the German car beat 0578M by 20.6sec after just over 3hr 23min of racing. The team was, as Antoine Prunet observed, 'dumbfounded'. All, that is, except Enzo Ferrari, who promptly signed up Gendebien.

● Inefficient Ferrari team management cost Eugenio Castellotti and 0578M victory in the Coppa D'Oro Delle Dolomiti. *(Current owner's archive)*

A Year in Italy

17 July 1955, L'Aosta-Gran San Bernardo hillclimb
Car number 164, Umberto Maglioli: **finished 1st.**
Chassis 0578M's next event was at the scene of another of Enzo Ferrari's 1921 successes, the Aosta-Gran San Bernardo hillclimb in the furthest north-west of Italy. It soared from 590m in the Aosta valley to 2470m above sea level, passing through Gignod, Etroubles and Saint-Rhemy. One of Ferrari's biographers, Gino Rancati credits him with victory on the event, although this was only in the 4,500cc class with a time of 37min 14sec. The overall winner on that occasion was Mercedes driver Ferdinand Minoia.

The tragic events of Le Mans cast doubt on the hillclimb for 1955, but it went ahead nonetheless with a new provision from the *Commissione Sportiva Automobilistica Italiana* that competitors would be banished from the results if they finished with bodywork or chassis damage from hitting trees, walls or other cars. Some 85 entries were received, with Umberto Maglioli reunited with 0578M considered one of the favourites. The car was refitted with a Tipo 119 3-litre engine and was also now using RIV telescopic shock absorbers instead of the usual hydraulic Houdaille ones.

In the event Maglioli went one better than Enzo Ferrari back in the 1920s. He not only won his class but also took a clear overall victory with a time of 22min 36.4sec (89.946kph) – a new record. Charging up the hill, he reached Etroubles in 9min 34.2sec, already beating Eugenio Castellotti's best time of the previous year, when the Ferrari team had been outshone by his 3.3-litre Lancia. He was eventually some 22sec quicker than the 1954 winner. Finishing second was new Ferrari recruit Gendebien, who had only two litres in his Mondial to take him to an exceptional finish time of 23min 38.1sec. Bordoni's Maserati was next in the rankings, followed by Swiss mountain champion Willy Daetwyler's 3-litre Ferrari. The following year, the latter won in a 750 Monza beating Maglioli in another 857S by over a minute, although Umberto's record remained intact.

● The victory for 0578M warranted this colour painting of the car in Alessandro and Massimo Acerbi's book on the L'Aosta-Gran San Bernado hillclimb.
Alessandro and Massimo Acerbi

European mountain climbing at its ● most challenging: 0578M kicks up the dust on the rough roads of the L'Aosta-Gran San Bernado contest.
The Klemantaski Collection/JJF Archive

Exceptional Cars

Olivier Gendebien

When it came to sports car racing, the aristocratic Belgian Olivier Gendebien had few peers during the late 1950s and early 1960s, in part thanks to an almost uncanny mechanical sympathy. 'He drives evenly, looks after his car and can be counted upon for clockwork precision in those races that call for steadfastness, character and common sense,' wrote Enzo Ferrari.

Gendebien first came to prominence in 1955 competing against, among others, 0578M in Italy. Having cut his teeth in rallying, he took part in his first sports car race in 1952, winning the Coupe de Spa the following season in a Ferrari 166MM. Two years later, he won the Coppa D'Oro Delle Dolomiti and the Liège-Rome-Liège Rally, driving a Mercedes-Benz 300SL. That brought an invitation from Ferrari to compete in the TT in one of the 857s, as they would become known. However, he crashed the original 0584M in practice.

His first full season with the *Scuderia* was 1956 but the following year he really started his impressive series of endurance race victories by winning a number of non-championship contests, most notably the Reims 12-hours. The 1958 season saw the first of his four Le Mans victories, partnering another who had driven 0578M: Phil Hill. This proved one of the most celebrated partnerships in endurance racing, the pair taking the 24-hour flagship race three times. He also won at La Sarthe in 1960, when he shared a Ferrari 250TR with compatriot Paul Frère, meaning a total of four victories there (three of them consecutive). Gendebien was the first ever to reach this total.

● Olivier Gendebien seems to have preferred jumping into his car the opposite side to other drivers. Here he practices such a start with 0578M at Buenos Aires.
The Klemantaski Collection/JJF Archive

The first of three Targa Florio wins also fell to him in 1958, to which can be added three consecutive Sebring 12-hours (two with Phil Hill) and the 1962 Nürburgring 1,000km.

Gendebien had less success as a Grand Prix driver, starting in just 14 World Championship counters, the majority in Ferraris. His best year in Formula One was 1960 when he drove a Cooper T51 for the Yeoman Credit-sponsored British Racing Partnership (BRP). He finished sixth in the table that year with a third in his home Grand Prix and a career best second in France, beaten by Jack Brabham but ahead of the Australian's factory Cooper team-mate Bruce McLaren following a frenetic battle. This also proved to be BRP's best result in a World Championship round. 'He was a gentleman, one of the few. "Jelly Bean" was no trouble, certainly not temperamental, and took everything in his stride,' says Tony Robinson, who was chief mechanic at BRP. Gendebien himself said Ferrari '…is a gentleman who never forgets that noblesse oblige.'

23 July 1955, 10 Ore Notturna Messinese
Car number 6, Eugenio Castellotti/Maurice Trintignant: **finished 1st.**

The nocturnal Dieci Ore Notturna Messinese was notable that year for its heavy number of retirements. Out of the 23 cars that started the 10-hour race 15 dropped out, but leading the survivors at the end was what the Ferrari archives now describe as 0578M, in its third win of the year. After its brief flirtation with 2-litre power, the car returned to being a 3-litre machine – the car never raced again with the smaller power unit. Castellotti returned to the driver's seat, this time accompanied by that year's Monaco Grand Prix winner Maurice Trintignant who was to enjoy the first of his two races with 0578M. Two others who had raced (or were soon to) 0578M, Maglioli and Dolomite winner Gendebien drove a sister car, but were forced to retire with gearbox failure. It is interesting to note that sharing the drive of Dan Margulies's Jaguar C-type was one Graham Hill, making his European sports car debut; the pair retired with a split fuel tank.

A Year in Italy

● (Left) Four rounds took place prior to 0578M's entry into the 1955 World Sports Car Championship. The first was at Buenos Aires where Maurice Trintignant and Froilán González (seen here at the wheel) retired this Ferrari 118 LM.
LAT Images

● (Left) A pair of Ferrari 750 Monzas at Le Mans in 1955: Mike Sparken's car, which he shared with Masten Gregory, leads that of 'Helde' and Jean Lucas.
The Revs Institute for Automotive Research/ George Phillips

● (Below) Piero Taruffi failed to finish the 1955 Mille Miglia with his Ferrari 118 LM. Two years later, this veteran of the event would win the last one held.
LAT Images

● (Above) The circus remained in America for the second round, the 12-Hours of Sebring. This is the Luigi Chinetti-entered Ferrari 750 Monza of Piero Taruffi and Harry Schell, which finished fifth.
The Revs Digital Library/Tom Burnside

Chapter 3
The Lanes of Ireland

Back in 1953, the International Sporting Commission (CSI) of the Federation International de l'Automobile (FIA) inaugurated a World Sportscar Championship. The World Drivers' Championship for Formula 1 had started three years earlier and now it was decided to introduce something similar to take in the major endurance races. Points were awarded on an eight, six, four, three, two, one basis for the first six cars, although only the first home from any manufacturer could count. While winning the Le Mans 24-hours remained the ultimate achievement for a sports car, the new championship became important in the 1950s, especially for Ferrari.

It narrowly wrested the first championship from Jaguar, although the British marque does not seem to have taken the contest seriously, and failed to send any cars to the final round. Ferrari won again in 1954 when the main challenger was Lancia, which it out-scored four victories to one.

A new contestant appeared for 1955, Mercedes-Benz, and it was trying to stop the German marque from winning the championship that a number of 750 Monzas, including 0578M, were reconfigured to become what were eventually known as 857S cars (as outlined in Chapter 1). It also meant that 0578M was elevated from relatively minor events on to the world stage of top-level racing.

The championship season started easily enough for Ferrari, which was almost the only European manufacturer to bother with the Buenos Aires 1,000km. The factory cars – a 750 Monza and a new six-cylinder 118 – were both disqualified during the race but there were enough privately-entered Ferraris around to secure the eight points. Jaguar took the Sebring 12-hours yet second place going to a Ferrari 750 Monza meant the Italians still led the championship. The Mercedes-Benz 300SLRs were at last out for the Mille Miglia, and with Stirling Moss scoring a legendary win for his new paymasters, the writing was on the wall for Ferrari. A variety of cars, including the potent six-cylinder 4.4-litre 121, had been used to contest the championship so far and for the next round, the Le Mans 24-hours, the *Scuderia* arrived with three of these. Eugenio Castellotti led the frenetic battle that filled the first hour of the race, only for his engine to give up the ghost. Much has been written about the horrific accident which occurred later on. To recap: confusion in front of the pit lane led to the 300SLR car of Pierre Levegh being catapulted into the crowd, causing the deaths of over 80 people; a number of major races were cancelled subsequently, including the next round of the World Sportscar Championship, the Nürburgring 1,000km. Round five would therefore take place in Ulster.

With hindsight we can now only wonder why – given how many other races had been cancelled in the wake of the Le Mans disaster – the 50th Tourist Trophy went ahead on such a potentially lethal circuit as Dundrod. Still, as *Autosport* pointed out: 'There does not seem to be any doubt but that the Ulster AC will hold the RAC Tourist Trophy at Dundrod on 17 September as planned', although '...the Race Committee will make a special inspection of the course with a view to tightening up on all safety measures.' Dundrod, it said, rather surprisingly, 'was relatively free from the safety problems which affected other circuits.'

The privately-entered Jaguar D-type of Bob Berry and Ninian Sanderson gets off first at the 1955 TT, followed by Hawthorn's factory car. Maglioli in 0578M is first away of the Ferrari drivers with Castellotti still to leave the line. The race would pan out very differently.
LAT Images

The Lanes of Ireland

- To the far right of the photo, Maglioli gets ready to mount 0578M (5), while Castellotti appears more energetic as he jumps into its sister car (4). Despite this, Umberto will leave the line first.
Grand Prix Library/Graham Gauld

17 September 1955, RAC Tourist Trophy, Dundrod, UK
Car number 5, Umberto Maglioli/Maurice Trintignant: finished 8th.

None of its cars had finished at Le Mans but Ferrari still led the championship because Mercedes-Benz had later withdrawn from the event following Levegh's crash. The Italian marque had 18 points, Jaguar 16, and Mercedes-Benz eight. However, many of these points were gathered by privately-entered cars, and the in-line six-cylinder engine had come to the end of the road. Apart from a 118 victory in the Tour of Sicily, it had suffered from one setback after another. Author Brock Yates wrote: 'By mid-1955, Ferrari's racing program (sic) was in a shambles'. The four-cylinder 500s and 750s had proved far more reliable and so Ferrari decided to revert to this configuration, albeit in a larger size. A 3,421cc four-cylinder, rated 280bhp at 5,800rpm, was mated to a four-speed gearbox and fitted to a 750 Monza chassis. Tests carried out at Monza and Mugello found the combination, was fairly satisfying, and three revised cars like this were entered for the TT. One was 0578M, to be driven again by Umberto Maglioli, this time partnered by Maurice Trintignant; the Frenchman won Le Mans in 1954 and had also won the '55 Monaco Grand Prix for Ferrari.

The 'new' cars were readily distinguishable from their 750 predecessors with larger, elliptical radiator grille

The Lanes of Ireland

The start of the 1955 Le Mans showing the privately entered Ferrari 750 Monza of 'Heldé' and Jean Lucas (12). To its left are the two cars that collided causing an horrific accident: Lance Macklin's Austin-Healey 100 (26) and the Mercedes-Benz 300SLR of 'Pierre Levegh' (20).
Daimler-Benz

opening, two long blisters on their bonnets, and sills that were upswept towards the rear. These sills already featured on Trintignant's 750 at the Supercortemaggiore Grand Prix.

The Tourist Trophy, first held in 1905, had relocated to the seven-mile long Dundrod circuit in 1950. The way the track was viewed may now raise eyebrows but was wholly indicative of the attitude of those times. Jaguar's competitions manager 'Lofty' England had earlier stated it was: 'The right type of circuit for the Tourist Trophy race, that is, a true road circuit, and which is definitely a driver's circuit. The only criticisms one might raise are that the road is somewhat narrow and that, by virtue of there being banks adjoining the road on the majority of the circuit, it is possible for the road to be obstructed if someone "prangs". This latter point, however, I feel has to be accepted as one of those things which must exist with a true road circuit.' By the end of the 1955 race, people would think very differently.

Nine miles from Belfast, the Dundrod circuit had an exposed locale, with high winds that proved yet another hazard. The first two TTs there had taken place on a smooth and comparatively non-abrasive, tarmac surface. Razor-sharp granite chips had been put down for 1953, probably to the delight of the tyre manufacturers.

New for 1955 was the fact that the pit area had been moved back. Finally, previous Ulster TTs had been handicap affairs but now the contest was a straightforward race.

Ferrari entered three of its revised 750s and was said by the media to be in 'a strong position'. Although all of these could be fitted with 3.5-litre engines, thanks to the bodywork changes it seems just one arrived in Northern Ireland with the larger power unit. The designation 857S comes from the engine's capacity per cylinder of 857.93cc. Given what happened at Dundrod, it is perhaps premature to refer to 0578M as such at this stage. Indeed, it seems this nomenclature did not come into use until the relevant cars, all now with 3.5-litre engines, were sold into private ownership.

During practice, the sole 3.5-litre engine gave trouble and was seen to be blowing out clouds of smoke. Olivier Gendebien, described even this early in his career as 'brilliant' by *Autosport* in its race preview, crashed at the deceptive wiggle that was Wheeler's Corner not long after training had started, badly damaging his car (0584M) and sustaining concussion and a broken arm. His co-driver Masten Gregory was subsequently loaned to Porsche. That left two cars, one driven by Maglioli and Trintignant, the other with Eugenio Castellotti and Piero Taruffi in charge. The first of these was reported to have telescopic shock absorbers

Maglioli's Ferrari is flanked at the start by the Cooper T38 (3) of the Whitehead brothers, one of whom will later acquire 0578M, and eventual winner, the Mercedes-Benz 300 SLR of Stirling Moss and John Fitch (10).
Current owner's archives

Ferrari 857S | 35

Umberto Maglioli

Pipe-smoking Italian Umberto Maglioli raced 0578M on five occasions, more than any other factory driver. Perhaps this is appropriate for he was best known as a sportscar driver – one of the foremost at genuine road racing - although he competed in 10 World Championship Grands Prix in which he twice made the podium with third places (both shared drives).

He joined *Scuderia* Ferrari in the middle of the 1953 season, having made his mark with a second place on the 1951 Mille Miglia and then victory in the 1953 Targa Florio, driving for Lancia both times. He won the daunting Sicilian race twice more in Porsches, sharing a 550 with Huschke von Hanstein in 1956 and a 907 with Vic Elford in 1968.

The son of a doctor, it was said that as he grew up he behaved and dressed exactly like one of that profession. Maglioli arrived at Ferrari at a time of change. After two years of World Championship domination, Alberto Ascari left the team to join Lancia for 1954, while Mercedes-Benz was also poised to enter the scene. For Ferrari, the good times in Grand Prix racing were temporarily at an end. The situation in endurance racing was, though, unchanged, and as author Cyril Posthumus wrote, it was a case of 'that horse again' in 1954.

Maglioli recalled that Enzo Ferrari was 55 when he first met him, and he was 25. 'You approached him with reverential fear, influenced because you saw everyone else treating him with great deference, careful not to irritate him.'

The 1954 World Sportscar Championship season commenced with a new round, the Buenos Aires 1,000km. The event was part of a collection of races in Argentina, collectively known as *Temporada* (The Season). Although the city boasted a modern and permanent circuit, it was felt this was not suitable for long-distance racing. So the Automobile Club of Argentina simply opened the gates of the Autodrome and extended the track out on to the fast motorway outside. The result was that cars would be travelling at high speed in opposite directions along the Avenida with just a central strip of grass and kerbs between them. It was touch and go whether Ferrari would even start the race, because its two 4.5-litre V12s and its new 3-litre, four cylinder model were held up by snow on the road from Modena to the docks at Genoa. In the end they had to be flown across the Atlantic. Maglioli was paired with 1950 World Champion Nino Farina in one of the V12s.

A cosmopolitan gaggle of cars shot away from the start, the leaders leaving Farina behind after he made a tardy getaway. Farina then got going 'seemingly,' in the words of Posthumus, 'under the impression that others should make way for his Ferrari.' Steering with one hand and waving his fist at the opposition with the other, he used the power of his V12 engine to storm past the others. After eight laps he was in front of the field, a lead he and Maglioli were never to lose, winning comfortably at an average speed of 93.43mph.

Even better was to come for Maglioli at the final round of the year, the fifth Carrera Panamericana in Mexico. This time he was driving alone. The entry was sadly lacking in factory cars of any sort but packed with potent, privately owned Ferraris. Two of these, the brutal 345bhp 4.9-litre cars that had been the class of Le Mans, were sold to the USA and Maglioli drove one for owner Erwin Goldschmidt. The 149-strong entry was despatched at one-minute intervals with Jack McAfee first off in the other 4.9-litre. About 100 miles north of the Tuxtla Gutierrez start, his Ferrari skidded over an embankment and, although McAfee escaped serious injury, his co-driver Ford Robinson died with a broken neck. Other Ferraris were dropping out fast but with, as Posthumus recorded, 'the wisdom of long experience', Maglioli refused to extend his car so early in the race. Phil Hill in his nimble 4.5-litre Ferrari and with Richie Ginther in the passenger seat, took over at the front, winning stage one from Umberto. The pair swapped placings on stage two, and then it was back to Hill in front of Maglioli for stage three. Maglioli then headed stages four, five, six and seven before Hill won the final, full-throttle blast across the desert. In summing up Maglioli's victory, an Italian friend told a reporter: 'He is something different. He is not wild. He does not eat much, he drinks less than he eats. He is not crazy over women; the head rules him. For a young Italian it is all very odd. For an Italian race driver it is nearly impossible.'

Maglioli himself would later comment: 'I considered the car like a living being and have always found it traumatic to maltreat a car. I think that, faced with the alternative of winning by over-revving or coming second, I would have been satisfied not to exceed the limit.'

Although he regarded his best performance to have been in the 1951 Mille Miglia driving a Lancia Aurelia (he finished second), Maglioli acknowledged that his name became linked to the Carrera Panamericana win. His performance in the middle of the race gave him overall victory but Hill's second place focussed the attention of Enzo Ferrari himself on the American's talents. In a few months both the protagonists in Mexico found themselves at the wheel of 0578M. Meanwhile, their efforts helped Ferrari to another World Sportscar Championship.

The following year saw another solo victory for Maglioli as he guided 0578M to victory on the Circuito del Mugello. As recorded elsewhere, it was one of five

times he drove the car that year, but he left Ferrari at the end of the season to be drafted into Porsche's sports car line-up during 1956. Around this time Stirling Moss noted in his diary that Maglioli had gone out with his then girlfriend Sally Weston. 'I was sure she was doing it just to piss me off,' said Sir Stirling later, observing that Maglioli was "a charming bloke, and quite good looking." He also said he was "as good as most in sports cars."

A crash at the Gaisburg hillclimb in Austria was to leave Maglioli with leg injuries so severe it was feared he would never walk again. However, he made an excellent recovery and in 1963 he returned to the Ferrari factory team, winning the Sebring 12-hours for the *Scuderia* the following season with Mike Parkes. His final successes were back with Porsche in 1968. Now 40 years old, his third Targa Florio win, and second in the same event the following year, again was with Elford. By this stage in his career, *Road & Track* magazine was describing him as 'venerated'.

● Not yet fit following a practice accident, Umberto Maglioli prepares to set off on the 1955 Mille Miglia driving a factory Ferrari 118LM. He was to finish third in the V6-engined car.
Cesare Martinengo

The Lanes of Ireland

installed, which underlines the belief that this was 0578M, the other car being 0570M.

Maglioli and Trintignant both took the wheel of 0578M during its practice – its headlights taped up with a striking star effect – with Gregory also putting in a couple of laps. None of them was as quick as Castellotti with the 3-litre Tipo 119 engine. By the time practice was over Ferrari had, as *Motor Sport* magazine reported, 'thrown away' the 3.5-litre motor and so both the remaining cars had 3-litre power.

As at Le Mans, the cars were lined up in echelon formation along the pit straight in order of engine capacity, not performance. It was, said *Motor Sport*, 'a thoroughly bad practice that should be stopped forthwith.' What this did mean was, as the 49 cars swept away from the start, three-abreast across the track, Maglioli found himself sandwiched between the Whitehead brothers' Cooper-Jaguar and Stirling Moss's Mercedes-Benz. And that was the last that Maglioli saw of Moss. The Englishman carved through cars in front of him and was easily leading at the end of the first of the 84 laps. As the cars flashed past the pits for the first time, Maglioli was back in eighth place.

Unfortunately, the two Ferraris – 'a trifle scruffy in appearance,' said the media – were not in the same league as the three Mercedes-Benzes or the lone factory Jaguar D-type of Mike Hawthorn and Desmond Titterington. Indeed, for the three laps described by TT historian Richard Hough as 'uproarious', Castellotti was hounded by cheeky Colin Chapman's 1.1-litre Lotus-Climax Mark IX.

On the second lap, Dundrod's dangers came sharply into focus when Jim Mayers's Cooper T39 started a chain of events that saw more than six cars crash into (or near) its blazing wreck. The popular Mayers and the promising young Connaught driver Bill Smith were both killed.

The cars raced on and by the end of 10 laps Moss was leading Hawthorn by 47sec. Further down, Castellotti and Maglioli were battling with the Cooper of Peter Whitehead; this man would feature in 0578M's future.

● The Castellotti/Taruffi 857S leads the sister car of Maglioli/Trintignant around Dundrod's first gear hairpin. The Dundrod circuit, over which they race, was situated about nine miles from Belfast and had first been used for the TT in 1950. Its drawbacks were an exposed locale, which caused winds to be a danger to the lighter cars, and its high, view-obstructing banks.
LAT Images

The sister Ferrari to 0578M, Castellotti's 0570M displays the results of his spin at Leathemstown.
LAT Images

Maurice Trintignant

Maurice Trintignant, the son of a wealthy vineyard owner and a recipient of the Legion d'Honneur, began his involvement in motor sport as mechanic to his older brothers. *LAT Images*

Maurice Trintignant's race-winning career spanned what might be described as three eras. His victories at Chimay in 1938 and 1939 were achieved driving a Bugatti Type 51, the classical looks of which were already outdated. The first of his two World Championship Grand Prix wins, that at Monte Carlo in 1955, was with a factory Ferrari that epitomised the front-engined racers of the 1950s while his second Monaco GP win three years later was at the wheel of Rob Walker's Cooper-Climax, the rear-engined configuration which was rapidly to become the norm.

Those Monaco wins made Trintignant, as far as World Championship statistics were concerned, the most successful French driver of the 1950s and 1960s, although never the greatest – that was surely Jean Behra. The French had invented motor racing and, for years, supplied many of its top drivers. In the 1940s, Jean-Pierre Wimille was widely regarded as the best of his time. But his death in a minor event the season before the start of the first World Championship saw France robbed of the chance to win the ultimate title, something it would have to wait until 1985 to enjoy. Nevertheless, Trintignant did his best, finishing fourth in the series in both 1954 and 1955, although both his GP victories were 'inherited'. He appeared in every one of the World Championships' first 15 seasons, starting with a factory Gordini at Monte Carlo in 1950 and finishing with his own BRM in Italy.

Trintignant also had his successes in sports cars, which included the win at Messina in 0578M. Most notable was victory at Le Mans in 1954, when he and José Froilán González led throughout for Ferrari.

He carried the soubriquet 'Le Petoulet' (rat droppings) given to him by Wimille after his retirement from the 1945 Coupe de la Libération. His Bugatti ground to a halt that day with fuel starvation caused by rats that had nested in its tank during the Second World War, during which it had been hidden in a haystack. He was, noted Stirling Moss: 'Always very charming and amusing. Competent rather then flash. He won Monaco, which tells you he was a precise driver.'

The Lanes of Ireland

(Above) Umberto Maglioli presses on to eighth place in 0578M.
Grand Prix Library/ Graham Gauld

(Above, right) Seen here well prepared for Irish weather, Eugenio Castellotti was to drive 0578M on a number of occasions. However, at Dundrod, he was at the wheel of 0570M.
Current owner's archives

On the 14th lap Whitehead overtook Maglioli and at midday, after one-and-a-half hours of racing, 0578M was in ninth place, still behind Whitehead (who eventually retired with a broken chassis) but leading the Ferraris of Jacques Swaters and Castellotti.

The latter spun at Leathemstown, battering the side of his Ferrari, which meant a lengthy pit stop to straighten it out and the chance for Chapman to get on his tail. Castellotti eventually rid himself of the 'embarrassing little green Lotus' but now the Ferraris were behind not only the Mercedes-Benzes and the lone Jaguar but also two Maseratis and a couple of Aston Martins. A violent puncture catapulted Moss into the banks, necessitating a trip to the pits to tear away damaged bodywork and replace the rear tyres. Hawthorn and Titterington were now well ahead of the field but rain then started to fall, and once Moss had regained the wheel from co-driver John Fitch he began relentlessly to haul in Titterington. As for the Ferraris, not long after 1.30pm Maglioli handed over to Trintignant, and Castellotti to Taruffi.

Tragically, a little Elva-Climax overturned at Tornagrough, catching fire and killing its driver Richard Mainwaring, the third fatality of the race. The mercurial Jean Behra also crashed; he lost his right ear, which was severed by a lens from the spare goggles hanging around his neck. As a result he wore a prosthetic ear for the rest of his life. In reporting these gruesome moments, a section of the popular press, in the words of *Autosport*: 'Reached a new low standard of common decency'. But not surprisingly, the TT never returned to Dundrod. Meanwhile Moss regained the lead, briefly lost it again during pit stops, and eventually surged on to victory. Within a quarter of an hour from the finish the still battling Hawthorn was forced to abandon the race with a blown engine.

What of the Ferraris? 0578M finished eighth, two places behind its stablemate. Its fastest lap (its 23rd) had been 5min 0secs (88.40mph), a full 18sec slower than the best, recorded by the Hawthorn/Titterington Jaguar. As far as a new Index of Performance formula was concerned, it was even further behind, 16th with a score of 0.91566 (the complex formula took the speed of each car multiplied by its engine capacity, plus 240, or the capacity multiplied by 97). Ferrari was outclassed once again.

The Lanes of Ireland

Trintignant, the winner of the previous year's Le Mans 24-Hours, could only finish eighth at the 1955 Tourist Trophy with 0578M.
Grand Prix Library/Graham Gauld

18 September 1955, RAC Tourist Trophy, Dundrod, UK

Round 5 World Sportscar Championship

1	*Stirling Moss (GB)/John Fitch (USA)*	Mercedes-Benz 300 SLR	84 laps
2	*Juan Manuel Fangio (RA)/Karl Kling (D)*	Mercedes-Benz 300 SLR	83 laps
3	*Wolfgang von Trips (D)/André Simon (F)/Karl Kling (D)*	Mercedes-Benz 300 SLR	82 laps
4	*Peter Walker (GB)/Dennis Poore (GB)*	Aston Martin DB3S	81 laps
5	*Luigi Musso (I)/Franco Bordoni (I)*	Maserati 300S	79 laps
6	*Eugenio Castellotti (I)/Piero Taruffi (I)*	Ferrari 857S	79 laps
7	*Reg Parnell (GB)/Roy Salvadori (GB)*	Aston Martin DB3S	79 laps
8	*Umberto Maglioli (I)/Maurice Trintignant (I)*	Ferrari 857S (0578M)	79 laps
9	*Carroll Shelby (USA)/Masten Gregory (USA)*	Porsche 550 Spyder	75 laps
10	*Michael MacDowel (GB)/Ivor Bueb (GB)*	Cooper-Climax T39	74 laps

- (Far left) Lance Macklin, who had been involved in the Le Mans tragedy, heads Trintignant in practice at Dundrod.
The Revs Institute for Automotive Research

(Left) The narrow lanes of the Irish circuit were to underline motor sport's potentially lethal nature.
The Revs Institute for Automotive Research/George Phillips

Chapter 4
Subdued in Sicily

With the Carrera Panamericana, like the Nürburgring 1,000km, cancelled following the Le Mans tragedy, just one round remained for Ferrari to try and retain the World Sportscar Championship. It still led the field with 19 points, compared to the 16 of both Mercedes-Benz and Jaguar. That the latter was not really interested in the title was clear from its single entry for the TT, so Jaguar was hardly likely to bother with the 39th Targa Florio, a circuit totally unsuited anyway to its D-type. Mercedes-Benz, on the other hand, was serious about the award, having already taken the World Drivers' title and the European Rally Championship. Now, it wanted the hat trick.

16 October 1955, Targa Florio, Sicily, Italy
Car number 120, Umberto Maglioli/Sergio Sighinolfi: retired.

This was Ferrari's second 'home race' of the series and it again brought two of the four-cylinder cars; the six-cylinders had obviously been abandoned. Progress had been made on the 3.5-litre engine because one was installed in the Eugenio Castellotti/Robert Manzon car, while Umberto Maglioli and his new partner Sergio Sighinolfi still had a 3-litre unit in 0578M. Since the Tourist Trophy a number of substantial suspension and chassis modifications had been made, with the engines moved forwards by 8cm to make the cars more stable. 'The improvement was striking,' wrote *Road & Track*'s Bernard Cahier, 'but the cars still lacked the superb Mercedes roadhandling.'

A third car was nominated for Piero Taruffi but this was apparently withdrawn after a quarrel. In the words of *Motor Sport* Continental Correspondent Denis Jenkinson: 'Mercedes-Benz went to Sicily in full force, while Ferrari did the best they could.'

Alfred Neubauer's men were digging deep to win the championship – Mercedes-Benz descended on Palermo with over 40 mechanics and six transporters. To the 21st century motor racing mind, this may not seem noteworthy but in 1955 it was a sign of real intent. Mercedes also had 15 sports-racing and touring cars on hand, and at least three shortwave mobile radio stations. To ensure everyone was well tucked-up for the night before the race, accommodation was booked within a 5km radius of the start. The planning was all the more impressive when one considers team manager Neubauer had, until virtually the last minute, been under the impression the race had been cancelled in the wake of Le Mans. Still, one French privateer turned up towing his sports Renault behind a saloon car, with no co-driver, no mechanics and just, as Cahier put it, 'two charming ladies'.

By contrast, reporter Salvatore Catania reckoned the approach of: '*Scuderia* Ferrari to this very important race seemed rather amateurish compared to that of the Stuttgart team; during the race itself it was obvious that those in charge of the Ferraris were either unaware of the cars' fuel consumption or of the tank capacity.' For its three cars, Ferrari employed a mere six mechanics.

Although the laps were shorter than when the race was first run in 1906, there were still 72km per circuit of the Madonie route (the actual number of laps had increased from eight to 13). One of the straights was an epic 4km long, and there were said to be over 10,000

Viva Castellotti e Maglioli! Eugenio, who had driven 0578M earlier in the season and Umberto, who was again behind its wheel during the Targa Florio, were obviously popular with the Sicilian locals. Here Eugenio speeds past with its sister car, 0570M.
Getty Images/Bernard Cahier

Subdued in Sicily

curves to negotiate. Crowd control was non-existent. As *Autosport* editor Gregor Grant pointed out that year, sudden storms, landslides of mud and rock, and parts of the road that had simply disintegrated were just some of the hazards drivers faced. Recent bad weather made matters even worse, with local labourers working tirelessly during the days beforehand to try and keep the roads clear.

Because of the late-year scheduling, the entry was perhaps slimmer in quality than previous Targas, but there was still a 'rich list' of native Sicilians in all manner of machinery. However, the organisers under the guidance of event founder Vincenzo Florio disallowed sports cars under 750cc and Gran Turismo vehicles of less than 1.1-litre.

Such was the nature of the Targa Florio course – *Autosport* described it as 'mountain-racing' – that the cars were sent off singly and 0578M, with Maglioli driving, was the last to leave the starting line departing, said *The Autocar*'s WF Bradley: 'In a burst of glory'.

Castellotti in 0578M's stablemate was two places ahead of Maglioli on the road, the pair sandwiching a Maserati. Early on, Umberto settled into eighth place, moving up to seventh by the fourth lap, and was reported to be 'strangely subdued'.

Stirling Moss set his customary cracking pace until he slid on some mud, shot into a field, and nearly plunged over a precipice. Local farm workers manhandled his Mercedes-Benz back on to the road and in the direction of the pits, and Moss had to retrieve the crash helmet that had blown off as he accelerated away. Peter Collins then took over the mangled Mercedes while the wild Castellotti now moved into the lead for Ferrari. He soon refuelled and handed over to Manzon. The Italian was appreciably quicker in the heat than his French teammate but the pair continued to mix it with the three Mercedes cars. Near Caltavoltura a tyre burst while Manzon was at the wheel. He changed this out on the

● Castellotti closes in on the Titterington/Fitch Mercedes-Benz. He and Manzon finished third with 0570M, splitting the German cars and beating the Irish/American pairing. *Daimler-Benz*

Sergio Sighinolfi

Sergio Sighinolfi's part in the story of 0578M is a fleeting one, sharing the car with Umberto Maglioli in the 1955 Targa Florio. Hailing from Modena, he was hired by Ferrari as a test driver in 1953 following his performances mainly with a Stanguellini S1100 that resulted in wins at Modena in 1950 and in the 1.1-litre Coppa d'Oro di Sicilia the following year.

Although he is said to have been entered as a substitute driver for Piero Carini's *Scuderia* Marzotto Ferrari for the 1952 French Grand Prix, he never competed at World Championship level. The main single-seater races that year were for Formula Two and, in one of these, the Gran Premio di Napoli, he crashed his Ferrari on the 50th lap and was unclassified. Later that year Sighinolfi shared a Ferrari 500 with Alberto Ascari at the Gran Premio di Modena, the pair finishing third behind Luigi Villoresi (Ferrari) and José Froilán González (Maserati).

While he competed in over 30 races during his career, his time with *Scuderia* Ferrari seems to have resulted in only three major sports car contests: he finished second driving a 500 Mondial on the 1954 2-litre Circuito de Senigalia behind Luigi Musso's Maserati; sixth the following year on the Mille Miglia with 750 Monza 0486M; and the 1955 Targa Florio with 0578M.

The following year he was killed after he crashed into a truck while testing a Ferrari 250 Europa on a public road at San Venanzio, between Modena and Maranello.

● Sergio Sighinolfi drove this Ferrari 750 Monza on the 1955 Mille Miglia, finishing sixth. The Targa Florio was his only other major endurance race that year. Four years earlier, he had been successful in Sicily with a win on the Coppa d'Oro di Sicilia in his Stanguellini S1100. *LAT Images*

road but then drove to the pits after which, 'amid wild screams of joy' from the enormous crowd lining the circuit, a fuming Castellotti – who had literally dragged Manzon out of the car – set off for the last two laps. Such was his anxiety to be back in the fray that he tried to drive off with the rear wheels still jacked up and the fuel funnel still sticking out of the tank.

The Moss/Collins and Juan Manuel Fangio/Karl Kling cars now led, positions they maintained until the end, but Eugenio Castelotti could still pip the Mercedes of the consistent Desmond Titterington and American John Fitch to get home third. Gregor Grant reckoned Ferrari threw away the Championship by misjudging the number of laps Castellotti and Manzon had behind the wheel. The regulations stated no driver could remain *in situ* for more than six laps, and the miscalculation meant much time was lost when Castellotti had to hand over to Manzon for a single lap.

Ferrari 0578M was overshadowed by its stablemate that day and was never in the picture, retiring on the last lap with a lost wheel. It was the car's only retirement that season. 'Maglioli and Sighinolfi were not really in the picture with the other works Ferrari,' wrote Grant in his later summing-up.

'Maglioli and Sighinolfi were not really in the picture with the other works Ferrari,' wrote Gregor Grant in his later summing up. However, Castellotti and Manzon certainly were, mixing it with the Mercedes team in number 116.
The Klemantaski Collection/ JJF Archive

The Castellotti/Manzon 857S pits in Sicily. *Autosport* editor, Gregor Grant believed that Ferrari threw away chances by miscalculating when these took place.
The Klemantaski Collection/ JJF Archive

16 October 1955, Targa Florio, Sicily, Italy

Round 6 World Sportscar Championship

1	Stirling Moss (GB)/Peter Collins (GB)	Mercedes-Benz 300 SLR	13 laps
2	Juan Manuel Fangio (RA)/Karl Kling (D)	Mercedes-Benz 300SLR	13 laps
3	Eugenio Castellotti (I)/Robert Manzon (F)	Ferrari 857S	13 laps
4	Desmond Titterington (GB)/John Fitch (USA)	Mercedes-Benz 300SLR	13 laps
5	Carlo Manzini (I)/Francesco Giardini (I)	Maserati A6GCS	13 laps
6	Giuseppe Musso (I)/Giuseppe Rossi (I)	Maserati A6GCS	13 laps
7	Giulio Cabianca (I)/Piero Carini (I)	Osca MT4 1500	13 laps
8	Giorgio Scarlatti (I)/Osbvaldo Lippi (I)	Maserati A6GCS	13 laps
9	Luigi Bellucci (I)/Maria Teresa de Filippis (I)	Maserati A6GCS/53	13 laps
10	Gaetano Starrabba (I)/Salvatore La Pira (I)	Maserati A6GCS	12 laps
And…	Umberto Maglioli (I)/Sergio Sighinolfi (I)	Ferrari 857S (0578M)	10 laps (retired)

Subdued in Sicily

● Writing in *Road & Track*, Bernard Cahier reckoned that the 1955 Targa Florio showed 'Castellotti is gaining more and more the qualities necessary to make a new world champion.' He had 'driven an inferior car with admirable courage.'
Getty Images/Bernard Cahier

Eugenio Castellotti

Three of the first four World Championships had fallen to Italian drivers but, with the death of Alberto Ascari early in 1955, the country was now anxious for a successor to take back the title. What better direction to look than towards Eugenio Castellotti, who had been Ascari's teammate at Lancia?

Of humble origins (unlike Italy's other new hope Luigi Musso), Eugenio had first attracted attention in 1952 when he had been driving a Ferrari for Scuderia Guastalla. That year the Monaco Grand Prix was contested by sports cars. Following a multiple accident, which eliminated the leaders, Castellotti found himself at the front. He fell back behind Vittorio Marzotto's Ferrari following a halt for fuel. A later fuel stop was much slower than that of his rival, and that margin left him in second. He was also a class winner on the Giro di Sicilia and then won races at Porto and Syracuse. He went on to finish third on the 1953 Carrera Panamericana and 1954 Tourist Trophy, winning the Italian hillclimb championship both years.

The usually yellow-shirted Castellotti had been driving sports cars for Lancia since late 1953. The manufacturer entered the Formula One arena towards the end of 1954 and for the start of the following season it included Eugenio alongside the great Alberto Ascari in its Grand Prix team. He crashed in the extreme heat in Argentina but then finished second in Monaco. That, though, was the race where Ascari finished up in the harbour and, within a week, had perished testing a 750 at Monza (see Chapter 2). Lancia withdrew from the scene although Castellotti persuaded it to let him have a car for the Belgian Grand Prix, where he was the sensation of practice, putting it on pole ahead of the works Mercedes-Benz of Juan Manuel Fangio and Stirling Moss; sadly, he retired in the race itself with a split gearbox. Despite this gallant appearance, Lancia was firmly resolved to finish with racing; what might have happened to Castellotti's career had it not done so is anyone's guess.

The move to Ferrari for the rest of the 1955 season was probably logical. A fifth in Holland and then third in Italy helped him to third overall in the World Championship table, well behind the all-conquering Mercedes-Benz twins. He stayed with the *Scuderia* after Lancia's racing programme was transferred to the Ferrari team for 1956. It was the year of his greatest victory: a win on the Mille Miglia during which he was said to have showed indomitable courage in appalling weather. He also won at Sebring that year, partnering Fangio. At Reims, he mirrored his best ever Grand Prix result by finishing second, but he was reportedly frequently 'over-driving', which often led to retirement.

● Eugenio Castellotti is seen here at Mugello. Much was expected of him by the Italian nation but, although he came first in the 1956 Sebring and Mille Miglia and 1957 Buenos Aires endurance contests, he was never to win a World Championship Formula One Grand Prix. *Current owner's archives*

Rivalry with teammate Musso was more likely to lead to his undoing. At Monza, for example, he retired due to tyre failure following a high-speed battle. For four laps, the pair fought to prove to their countrymen who was the greater, despite boards shown in frustration from the Ferrari pit exhorting them to slow down. Their Ferrari colleagues Fangio and Peter Collins sat back and awaited the inevitable…

Castellotti's final victory was in the 1957 Buenos Aires 1,000km, sharing a Ferrari 290MM with Masten Gregory and the aforementioned Musso. Enzo Ferrari then recalled him from a holiday he was enjoying in Florence with attractive actress Delia Scala to test a new Formula One car at Modena. Some feel Ferrari was callous in the way in which he summoned Eugenio, who set off at around 5am for the track. Jean Behra was also testing at Modena with a Maserati 250F and Ferrari was anxious his cars should not lose the track record there.

Il Commendatore later wrote, controversially, that Castellotti was then: 'going through a confused and conflicting time emotionally', saying this may have caused 'a momentary slowness in his reactions'. Whatever the truth, Castellotti crashed and the car rolled into a grandstand with the driver being thrown out, his body striking a concrete post. He died from the resulting severe head injuries. It was, wrote Ferrari: 'A banal accident'. Veteran driver Luigi Villoresi, though, said it was the result of 'Ferrari's pride'.

Italy still awaits Ascari's successor.

Chapter 5
Factory finale in America

Having been used for the final two races of the 1955 World Sportscar Championship, 0578M continued to be a factory weapon of choice for the opening American rounds of the following year's series, the Buenos Aires 1,000km and the 12 Hours of Sebring.

29 January 1956, 1,000km of Buenos Aires
Car number 36, Olivier Gendebien/Phil Hill: **finished 2nd.**
Now fitted with the 3.5-litre Tipo 129 engine, the car travelled to Argentina for what was to be its finest hour. With Mercedes-Benz having withdrawn from the fray, Ferrari was anxious to regain its dominance and sent a pair of 4.9-litre cars to Buenos Aires, in addition to 0578M, which was to be driven by new team members Olivier Gendebien and Phil Hill, a partnership that would become legendary in endurance racing in the years to come – especially at Le Mans. Back-up for the *Scuderia* came from a privately entered 4.9-litre and two 4.5-litres.

The previous year the organisers had used a fast 10.56-mile version of the Autodrome-cum-motorway circuit introduced in 1954 (see Umberto Maglioli section, Chapter 3). For 1956 the theme was the same, with a return to the 5.88-mile lap, but run clockwise just to be different.

Following a traditional Le Mans start 0578M shot off into a shortlived lead before the 4.9s gobbled their way to the front. By the end of 20 laps, 0578M driven by Gendebien was back to fourth behind its two stablemates and the Maserati Stirling Moss was sharing with Carlos Menditéguy. The race continued with little change in the positions, the gaps opening up until the pit stops revived the earlier excitement of the race. Luigi Musso (Ferrari

4.9-litre) took the lead when Juan Manuel Fangio handed over to Eugenio Castellotti, and then Moss moved to the front as Musso was replaced by Peter Collins.

Castellotti then hit some straw bales and bent a wheel, dropping his car back to fifth. It was also reported that he hit one of the dogs that seemed to plague the event, although it is unclear if this was in fact the same accident. The Collins/Musso Ferrari was now at the front, harried by the 3-litre Maserati. By the 60-lap mark Hill was in third place in 0578M headed only by these two. When the leader dropped out on the 68th lap with a broken rear axle, the Maserati strode into first place, while Ferrari's new racing manager Eraldo Sculati hastily flagged in Castellotti and replaced him with Fangio. The World Champion hauled his compatriot Menditéguy in fast. Maserati also had a new team manager, former Ferrari man Nello Ugolini, who responded by putting Moss back in the car.

● Gendebien accelerates into a shortlived lead at Buenos Aires with 0578M. The V12 Ferraris of Juan Manuel Fangio/Eugenio Castellotti (43) and Enrique Saenz Valiente/Jorge Camano (45) are also off the mark, while Luigi Musso in the second factory 410 Sport has yet to get away.
whitefly.cc

V12 and four-cylinder Ferraris ● leave the line at Buenos Aires, Luigi Musso's 4.9-litre on the left, Olivier Gendebien's 0578M on the right. Some 104 laps later, the latter was to finish second, its best ever result in a World Championship race.
The Hill family archives

Factory finale in America

Ferrari 857S | 53

Factory finale in America

With 20 laps left, it looked as if Fangio might overhaul Moss. However, his chase was all in vain when the differential broke on the second of the big Ferraris on the 90th of 106 laps. *Autosport* magazine described the event as 'a race of destruction'.

This meant that in second place was now the 3.5-litre 0578M, a position it retained to the end – two laps back from the winner after nearly six-and-a-half hours of racing – to give Ferrari six points towards the Championship. Thanks to the Moss/Menditéguy Maserati having a smaller engine, 0578M also took the Over 3-litre class. The larger four-cylinder Ferrari engine had now started to perform as expected and was proving reliable.

Ferrari 857S chassis 0578M may have won at a lower level but this was surely the high point of its career. Having said that, the Prancing Horse had been prodded by the Trident which now led the Championship at eight points to the six scored by 0578M.

One of the truly great partnerships of endurance racing, Olivier Gendebien (left) and Phil Hill, shared 0578M at Buenos Aires. Thrice, they were to pair up to win the Le Mans 24-hours.
The Klemantaski Collection/ JJF Archive

19 January 1956, Buenos Aires 1,000km, Argentina

Round 1 World Sportscar Championship

1	*Stirling Moss (GB)/Carlos Menditéguy (RA)*	Maserati 300S	106 laps
2	*Olivier Gendebien (B)/Phil Hill (USA)*	Ferrari 857S (0578M)	104 laps
3	*Jean Behra (F)/José Froilán González (RA)*	Maserati 300S	101 laps
4	*Alejandro de Tomaso (RA)/Carlo Tomasi (RA)*	Maserati 150S	97 laps
5	*Enrique Muro (YV)/Julio Pola (YV)*	Ferrari 500 Mondial	93 laps
6	*Eduardo Kovacs-Jones (RCH)/Raul Jaras (RCH)*	Mercedes-Benz 300SL	90 laps
7	*Isabell Haskell (USA)/Carlos Lostalo (RA)*	Maserati 150S	88 laps
8	*Angel Maiocchi (RA)/Lucio Bollaert (RA)*	Ferrari 225S	85 laps
9	*Franco Bruno (RA)/Carlos Bruno (RA)*	Allard J2 Cadillac	71 laps

Chassis 0578M makes a pit stop during the Buenos Aires 1,000km.
The Klemantaski Collection/ JJF Archive

Exceptional Cars

Factory finale in America

● (Above) As the larger engined Ferraris dropped out of contention, so 0578M moved up to an eventual second place at Buenos Aires.
The Klemantaski Collection/JJF Archive

● (Below) Cars on board ship on their way to Buenos Aires with the 0587S parked at right angles to the rest.
whitefly.cc

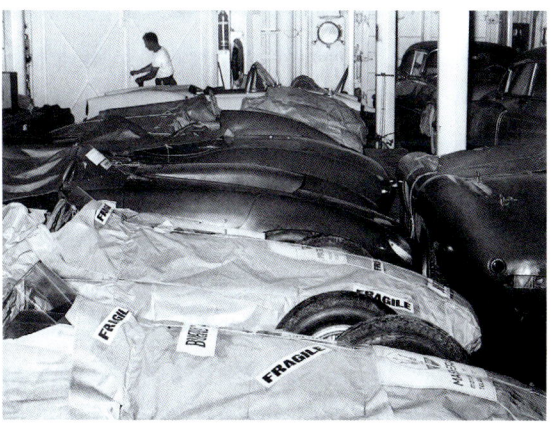

Ferrari 857S

Factory finale in America

Factory finale in America

- (Left) Phil Hill, who had made his Ferrari factory debut the previous year, started the season in fine style, taking 0578M to second place at Buenos Aires with Olivier Gendebien.
The Klemantaski Collection/ JJF Archive

- (Right) The 3.5-litre 0578M was the smallest of the three works Ferraris at Buenos Aires. However, it was the only one that finished and the day has to be said to have belonged to Maserati.
whitefly.cc

- (Left) 'Menacing heat and the mixed quality of the entry combined to keeping the stands half empty,' wrote Autosport's Dr Vincente Alvarez in 1955. They still did not seem to have filled up the following year.
The Klemantaski Collection/ JJF Archive

Ferrari 857S | 57

Factory finale in America

24 March 1956, 12 Hours of Sebring, Florida, USA
Car number 19, Alfonso de Portago/Jim Kimberly: **retired.**
Sebring remains to this day obviously an airfield circuit but by 1956 its 12-hour race was on its way to becoming one of the premier events on the endurance racing calendar. Its Floridian location may have seemed far from the European centre of sports car racing but the race attracted a healthy entry from Jaguar, Aston Martin, Maserati, Porsche and even Lotus.

Ferrari left its 4.9-litre cars behind for the 12-hour race and was now relying solely on 3.5-litre fours. Three were entered, and one contemporary writer described them as 'new'. Indeed, two *were* brand new 860 Monzas. All three were listed in an internal report as simply '3500/4cl' but the third was 0578, obviously a 1955 machine. There was also a privately run 857S, Phil Hill sharing this white, George Tilp-entered car with Masten Gregory (chassis 0570M).

○ The factory Ferraris of (left to right) Fangio/Castellotti, Musso/Schell and Kimberly/de Portago line up at Sebring.
Current owner's archive

58 Exceptional Cars

24 March 1956, 12 Hours of Sebring, Florida, USA
Round 2 World Sportscar Championship

1	Juan Manuel Fangio (RA)/Eugenio Castellotti (I)	Ferrari 860 Monza	194 laps
2	Luigi Musso (I)/Harry Schell (USA)	Ferrari 860 Monza	192 laps
3	Bob Sweikert (USA)/Jack Ensley (USA)	Jaguar D-type	188 laps
4	Roy Salvadori (GB)/Carroll Shelby (USA)	Aston Martin DB3S	187 laps
5	Jean Behra (F)/Piero Taruffi (I)/ Cesare Perdisa (I)	Maserati 300S	186 laps
6	Hans Herrmann (D)/Wolfgang von Trips (D)	Porsche 550 Spyder	182 laps
7	Jack McAfee (USA)/Pete Lovely (USA)	Porsche 550 Spyder	179 laps
8	Alfonso Gomez-Mena (C)/Santiago Gonzalez (C)	Jaguar D-type	176 laps
9	John Fitch (USA)/Walt Hansgen (USA)	Chevrolet Corvette Special	176 laps
10	Porfirio Rubirosa (DR)/Jim Pauley (USA)	Ferrari 500 Mondial II	172 laps
And	Jim Kimberly (USA)/Alfonso de Portago (E)	Ferrari 857S (0578M)	137 laps, retired

● By 1956, Ferrari 857S chassis number 0570M was in private hands. Phil Hill, who had driven 0578M at the previous World Championship round, Buenos Aires, shared the car with (seen here) Masten Gregory at Sebring. *Getty Images/Bernard Cahier*

● (left) Mike Hawthorn (8) leaves the line first at Sebring in one of the D-types entered by New York Jaguar distributor Briggs Cunningham. Thanks to their smaller capacity engines, the factory Ferraris are still way back. *Getty Images/Bettman*

Once again, 0578 had a different pair of drivers, factory new boy Alfonso de Portago and Jim Kimberly. It was the only time Kimberly raced a factory Ferrari and he may have been given the drive because of gearbox trouble he was having with his own 121LM in practice. With grid positions allotted on engine size due to a lack of qualifying sessions, Kimberly should have started in third position in the 4.4-litre car he was to share with Ed Linken.

Before a crowd of around 25,000, the two 860s driven by Juan Manual Fangio/Eugenio Castellotti and Luigi Musso/Harry Schell respectively ran out first and second, but for 0578 there was no repeat of the Buenos Aires glory. Its Tipo 129 engine was over-revved to 6,600rpm and a suspected broken valve ended the car's final World Championship race on its 136th lap. An internal report showed that the winning car had only recorded 6,100rpm on the telltale.

Factory finale in America

The car was lying in seventh place at the end of the first hour with de Portago still at the wheel, moving up to fifth by 1pm thanks to retirements and pit stops. An hour later and the ranking was identical but shortly afterwards Kimberly managed a double spin at the first turn, missing three other cars during his gyrations and falling back down the order. From then on 0578M ceased to be in any form of contention, with eventual retirement coming in the seventh hour. Meanwhile, back in Europe, Peter Collins won the non-Championship Giro di Sicilia – one vast and gruelling 671-mile lap that hugged Sicily's rocky coast – in another Ferrari 857S, chassis 0584M. This number will come back to haunt us.

Chassis 0578M stayed in the USA and was displayed on the stand of Ferrari distributor Luigi Chinetti at the New York International Motor Show in late April/early May. A bump that it had received in Florida on the left hand front had been repaired and its Sebring number 19 replaced by the winning 17 of the 860 Monza of Fangio and Castellotti. Nobody was deceived and the car was still unsold at the conclusion of the exhibition.

● Sebring remains an airfield circuit to this day. Ferrari 0578M races past a Fairchild C-82 Packet cargo aeroplane in 1956.
The Revs Institute for Automotive Research/Tom Burnside

Alfonso de Portago

Ferrari 0578M's first year of racing was very much one of traditional road racing, charging on past solid hazards such as ancient buildings or deep ravines, the sides of the track often lined by hordes of unprotected, foolhardy spectators. It had been like this ever since the sport's founding fathers had thundered from one city to another; and it is a far cry from today's synthetic circuits with their run-off areas and safety fencing.

Two years later a tragedy occured that, while it did not bring an immediate end to genuine road racing – which would stagger on just into the 1970s – it was almost certainly the beginning of the end. One of those who had driven 0578M as a factory car was closely involved at this turning point.

The flamboyant Spanish nobleman Alfonso de Portago and his American passenger Ed Nelson were pressing on at over 150mph with their Ferrari 335S during the 1957 Mille Miglia. Then a left front Engelbert tyre burst, causing the car to somersault down the road. The car scythed out of control through the crowd, leaving 11 spectators dead – five of them children; de Portago and Nelson were killed too.

The Vatican and the Italian press were at once united in their condemnation of the sport. Enzo Ferrari contemplated quitting racing and, three days after the accident, the Italian government announced a ban on the Mille Miglia. It heralded the end for racing on mainland Italy's public roads.

Alfonso António Vicente Eduardo Angel Blas Francisco de Bonja Cabeza de Vaca y Leighton, Marquis de Portago could turn his hand to anything. He could speak four languages fluently,

● (Above) Alfonso de Portago races around Sebring's oil drums. The track was, some might say still is, spartan in character. *Current owner's archive*

his sexual liaisons were legendary, he qualified as a pilot aged just 17 and, he was accomplished at a variety of sports. For most, finishing fourth in the 1956 Olympics two-man bobsleigh or thrice being amateur steeplechase champion of France (he even rode in the Grand National at Aintree, twice) might be sufficient. But 'Fon' also competed at tennis, skiing and boxing …and he was not bad at racing cars.

He had just become a member of the Ferrari factory team when he drove 0578M at Sebring.

● De Portago at Sebring in 1956. He was to crash fatally on the Mille Miglia the next year, effectively bringing an end to that great Italian endurance race. *The Revs Institute for Automotive Research/Tom Burnside*

Factory finale in America

Phil Hill

The Ferrari Formula One cars were so much more powerful than their rivals in 1961 that there was no doubt one of the *Scuderia*'s drivers, despite the heroics of Stirling Moss in a privately-entered Lotus 18, would win that year's World Championship. After series points leader Wolfgang von Trips crashed fatally at Monza, thoughtful, Florida-born but California-raised, Phil Hill moved up to take the title.

The following season Ferrari lost its edge, overshadowed by the new British V8 engines. Hill never won another Grand Prix. When it comes to single-seaters, none of the Ferrari class of '61 can be counted among the greats. However, as far as Hill was concerned, when it came to sports cars his name was up there with the best of them. His career path to a factory works drive was all about two-seaters as he progressed from an MG TC to an OSCA, with which he made his debut at Le Mans in 1953, and then with Ferraris entered by Allen Guiberson. Then his career really took off following second places in the 1954 Carrera Panamericana and 1955 Sebring 12-hours partnered by Richie Ginther and Carroll Shelby respectively.

The result was an invitation to drive a factory 735 LM at Le Mans in 1955, partnering Umberto Maglioli. The pair made an excellent start and was up to third after the first three hours before retiring with clutch failure. He was then asked to join the *Scuderia* for the following year's World Sportscar Championship. Hence, as his first full season began as a Ferrari works driver, Hill was driving 0578M for arguably its finest hour: the Buenos Aires 1,000km in which he and Olivier Gendebien finished second. By the end of the year he had scored his first victory in a Sportscar Championship round, the Swedish Grand Prix (with Maurice Trintignant) while his win (paired with Peter Collins) at the Venezuelan GP helped clinch the 1957 title for Ferrari. The track marking at Caracas was so poor that Hill in practice unwittingly found himself on the public roads and was 'just about at the point where I really began to wonder where the hell I was [when] all of a sudden there was a bunch of cars coming towards me! Sedans!'

Hill underlined his sports car expertise in 1958 by winning three of the first five rounds of the Sportscar Championship. At Le Mans he was reunited with Gendebien; a sublime partnership. Twice more in 1961 and 1962, the pair mounted the top step at La Sarthe. They were also together to win at Sebring in 1959 with Dan Gurney and Chuck Daigh. Other World Sportscar Championship races to fall to Hill were Buenos Aires (1960), Nürburgring (1962 and 1966), Daytona (1964) and Brands Hatch (1967).

It was not until towards the end of 1958, following the deaths of Luigi Musso and Peter Collins, that Phil was given the chance to race a Ferrari F1 car, proving his worth with a couple of third places in the final two races. Frustrated at waiting for that single-seater drive, earlier in the season he hired a Maserati 250F from Joakim Bonnier to make his Grand Prix debut. A couple of second places the following year were enough to place him fourth in the Championship with the first of three Grands Prix victories occurring at Monza at the end of 1960. This wrote him into the record books as the last driver to win a World Championship Grand Prix in a front-engined car.

Hill's relationship with Ferrari was far from harmonious. During 1962 team manager Eugenio Dragoni used Phil as a scapegoat for the fact that, two seasons into the new 1.5-litre Formula One, the British teams had caught up in the power stakes with the introduction of their V8 engines, and now had the quicker cars. Hill now made a career mistake, as did others, by throwing in his lot with the new and shambolic ATS team. From there he moved to Cooper, now on the slide down from its glory years. The American's F1 career was likewise on a steep decline and in 1966 he was more likely to be seen driving the camera car filming action sequences for the movie *Grand Prix*. A year later, though, he again proved his ability with a sports car, taking a high-winged Chaparral 2D-Chevrolet to victory in the BOAC Six Hours at Brands Hatch with Mike Spence.

Hill's prowess should not really be judged by his Grand Prix victories at Monza in 1960, when the race was boycotted by the leading British teams, or in Belgium and Italy the following season when Ferrari was the only team ready for the new regulations. Instead, it should be seen via his fantastic skills in two-seater endurance cars, with the drive in 0578M coming at a significant point in his career.

● Phil Hill as he is perhaps best remembered, in a 1.5-litre nostril-nosed Ferrari during 1961, the year of his World Championship.
LAT/David Phipps

Exceptional Cars

Factory finale in America

● Phil Hill partnered Olivier Gendebien to take 0578M to second place at Buenos Aires, its best result in a World Championship race. Here 0578M passes the stricken Austin-Healey 100M of Osvaldo Carballido.
The Klemantaski Collection/JJF Archive

Factory finale in America

Factory finale in America

- (Left) Improvements had been made to the Sebring track with a new bridge over the start, a new timing box and new fencing… but it was still primarily an airfield site.
The Revs Institute for Automotive Research/Tom Burnside

- (Right) Jim Kimberly lines 0578M up at Sebring. The track was particularly demanding on transmissions, brakes and engines.
The Revs Institute for Automotive Research/Tom Burnside

- (Below) Alfonso de Portago applies a touch of paint to his Ferrari 857S at Sebring in 1956.
The Revs Institute for Automotive Research/Tom Burnside

Ferrari 857S | 65

Factory finale in America

20 May 1956, Cumberland SCCA meeting, Maryland, USA
Car number unknown, Jack McAfee: **Did not start.**
Californian John Edgar already owned an 857S (chassis 0588M), which 'Big Jack' McAfee had first driven at Palm Springs in the February, winning with it at Stockton in the month before Sebring. He and Carroll Shelby were to drive it a number of times during 1956 and 1957, the future Le Mans 24-hours winner also taking it to victory at Montgomery in the August of the first year. Edgar, though, coveted one of the newer 860 Monzas. On 12 May he wrote to Enzo Ferrari enclosing a cheque 'for US$9,000 covering payment to you in full for the 3.5-litre car driven by Musso in the Sebring Grand Prix.' Antoine Prunet points out that Musso's car was still being campaigned by the factory while the other 860 Monza had already been sold to John von Neumann. There was no other 3.5-litre left from the Sebring race other than the 857S, 0578M. Chinetti was certainly happy to part with this and the car was rushed to Cumberland in Maryland for the Edgar team and McAfee to race in the SCCA meeting there on 20 May. After a few practice laps, the engine swallowed a valve. McAfee went on to win his race in Edgar's Porsche 550, but the owner was furious with Ferrari and cancelled the deal. His transporter dropped 0578M off in Indianapolis on its way back to Los Angeles. Chinetti was forced to have it collected from there and returned to Maranello.

● John Edgar already owned another 857S when Luigi Chinetti tried to sell him chassis 0578M. Jack McAfee drove this on a number of occasions including the 1956 Del Monte Trophy at Pebble Beach, where he finished third.
The Revs Institute for Automotive Research/Tom Burnside

Jim Kimberly

'Gentleman' Jim Kimberly enjoyed but one drive in a factory Ferrari, and even that may not have happened had he not been having trouble with his own Ferrari 121LM during practice for the 1955 12-hours of Sebring.

Instead of being paired to drive with Ed Linken, as he had there the previous year, he found himself sharing the seat of 0578M with 'Fon' de Portago.

The future president of the Sports Car Club of America (SCCA), paper-manufacturing heir Kimberly was a loyal adherent to the Ferrari marque. Among his long list of races, nearly all in North America, that stretched from the 1956 Sebring back to 1950, only two were in anything else. And unlike most of his compatriots, his relationship with Enzo Ferrari was cordial.

He fully epitomised the gentleman sportsman and it was certainly his belief that SCCA competition should be of an amateur nature. Having said that, he was ultra-professional in his approach not only to his racing – he was an SCCA National Champion – but also the way he ran the Club. It was a demeanour that made him one of the best-known drivers and officials of its early days.

● Jim Kimberly got his chance to drive 0578M at Sebring following the transmission failure of his own Ferrari 121LM during practice.
The Revs Institute for Automotive Research/Tom Burnside

Part 2
In private hands

● Its career as a factory-entered car over, '0578M/0584M', seen here (15) at Karlskoga in 1960, travelled the world in privateer hands. Following time in Australia and New Zealand, it returned to Europe and became part of the Scandinavia scene.
Orebro City Archives

During the 1950s the World Championships, both Formula One and Sportscars, were largely confined to Europe and the Americas. Far-flung regions such as Australia, New Zealand and South Africa developed their own series, starting in the main with *Formule Libre* in which local specials competed against an increasing amount of secondhand machinery from Europe. Eventually these metamorphosed into imitations of the European scene: South Africa with its own Formula One championship and the 'Down Under' countries with the Tasman series in which the cars differed from F1 only in the size of their engines.

The 1954 season is regarded as the one where motor racing came of age in New Zealand. That was the first year in which the locals found themselves up against an invasion of Europeans with relatively new cars. On the grid for the New Zealand Grand Prix could be seen a variety of machines, single-seaters and sports cars, that extended from a BRM V16 and three Cooper-Bristols to a Jaguar XK120 and a trio of Austin-Healey 100s, one of which was driven by local man Ross Jensen. A month later, Englishman Peter Whitehead scored the initial victory for a Ferrari in New Zealand when he came first in the Lady Wigram Trophy.

It was into an eclectic mix akin to this that Ferrari 857S chassis 0578M was sent following the end of its factory career. Over the next few years, it would journey from a one-off appearance in Australia during 1956, to a season in New Zealand, before returning to Europe to see out its contemporary career in Scandinavia.

Chapter 6
The other side of the world

It does not seem a bad business plan. Take a racing car 'Down Under', compete with it over the winter, and then sell it to a local before returning back to England. It mainly appears to have worked for sheep farmer and wool entrepreneur Peter Whitehead, who first competed on the other side of the world in 1938, winning the Australian Grand Prix – a handicap event that year – with his ERA B-type. Whitehead continued to race in the region during the early 1950s, winning the 1954 Lady Wigram Trophy in New Zealand in a Ferrari 125.

He returned to Australia in 1956 with the Ferrari that we have hitherto known as 0578M. Assembly forms show that some work was carried out on its return to the factory from the USA, and on 19 September it was stated that a 3-litre, Tipo 119 engine had replaced the Tipo 129 before being sold to Whitehead. It should perhaps be referred to as a 750 Monza during its 'Down Under' sojourn; this is certainly what the contemporary press called it.

To confuse matters, the cover page of the assembly forms shows the typewritten reference 0578M crossed out and replaced with a handwritten '0584M'. Ferrari historian Antoine Prunet points out this was a swap between two cars that were, at that point, unsold. 'The reason for the swap is unexplained,' states Prunet. 'It could be understood if it was a matter of customer's documentation – but it did create a lot of confusion among historians.'

25 November 1956, Australian Tourist Trophy, Albert Park, Australia *Car number 18, Peter Whitehead: finished 6th.*
In September 1956, 0578M, or '0584M' as we must call it for now, was sold to Whitehead. The Englishman then took both this and a Ferrari 555 Super Squalo single-seater to Australia to compete in events such as the country's own Grand Prix and its 100-mile Tourist Trophy, the latter on 25 November. The weather on race day was dull and threatening, following a particularly hot practice session the morning before. Television had just arrived in Australia, and this was the motor sport debut for a commercial station with cameras at three vantage points. The favourite Stirling Moss reckoned the 3.1-mile Albert Park circuit to be one of the best, even if some of the sections were rough.

The start was from a conventional grid after it was decided to abandon a Le Mans style getaway due to the comparatively narrow width of the road. Two 3-litre '750 Monza' Ferraris were in the field, the other one being driven by Ken Wharton. Also in the line up was New Zealander Ross Jensen in an Austin-Healey 100S. Moss was the class of the field in his Maserati 300S and on the 19th circuit he lapped Whitehead in '0584M' and was now 29sec ahead of his team mate Jean Behra. A couple of laps later Whitehead was reported to be in sixth place behind Moss, Behra, Wharton, and the Jaguar D-types of Bib Stilwell and Bill Pitt. Although dropping oil pressure caused Stilwell to slow sufficiently to fall behind Pitt, Whitehead was unable to benefit and remained in sixth to the very end, two laps behind the winner Moss. A couple of places further back was Jensen in his far less potent Austin-Healey, a fact that did not go unnoticed by Whitehead. (Incidentally, a short *Formule Libre* race also took place that weekend, which Whitehead won with his single-seater.)

● (Below) The start of the 1956 Australian TT with Peter Whitehead's '0578M/0584M' further back on the grid. Up front are Ken Wharton's similar 750 Monza (10) and the Maserati 300Ss of Stirling Moss (7) and Jean Behra (6). *LAT Images*

● The paddock at Armore Aerodrome in 1957. The *Formule Libre* nature of that year's New Zealand Grand Prix can be seen by the single seaters that surround '0578M/0584M' (18). In the foreground (5) is the Ferrari 550/860 that 0578M's owner, Peter Whitehead took to second place. Reg Parnell's similar car (4) was the winner that day.
Stenbeg Archive via Jim Barclay

The other side of the world

The other side of the world

Peter Whitehead

The chassis now known as '0548M' was then shipped to New Zealand for the start of 1957. Writer Graham Vercoe points out that Whitehead was already aware of Jensen's ability prior to the Australian TT but, following Ross's performance there, Whitehead negotiated a lease deal with the Auckland motor dealer to compete with it in his country's international series. Jensen said after that he found the handling of the car capricious, something he put down to a bent chassis. Ken Wharton entered in his similar car for the 1957 NZ season, both Ferraris being claimed at the time as 'ex-Castellotti' but perhaps that is like claiming a Maserati 250F is 'ex-Fangio'. The damaged chassis may have been the reason why Whitehead's car was described like that. Forty years later, as journalist Eoin Young recorded, Jensen reflected: 'It was a difficult car to drive. It tested one's mettle'.

12 January 1957, New Zealand Grand Prix, Ardmore, New Zealand *Car number 18, Ross Jensen:* **finished 4th.**
Whitehead, Wharton and Jensen were all entered for the fourth New Zealand Grand Prix, a *Formule Libre* affair at Ardmore Aerodrome (a typical ex-airfield venue with two wide runways and a taxiway) on 12 January. Peter was in his Super Squalo single-seater, Ken in his 250F and Ross in 0548M although, at the time of printing the event's programme, he was still expected to be driving his Austin-Healey.

Crowd favourite Wharton also chose to race his 750 Monza in the sports car race scheduled prior to the main event. Tragically, he was killed when his Ferrari, then leading the race, skidded and flipped upside down. The 50,000 spectators learnt of this just as the grid assembled for the GP, which had been changed from a race of two-and-a-half hours to three. According to Young, Jensen based a game-plan on this. In practice the extra laps would mean a pit stop for fuel. 'I calculated that if I increased the Monza's capacity by 10 gallons I could run non-stop to the finish'. The night before the

● Peter Whitehead and Ross Jensen stand between the latter's '0578M/0584M' and his Super Squalo at Ardmore.
Stenbeg Archive via Jim Barclay

Yorkshireman Peter Whitehead personified the amateur racing driver of the immediate post-Second World War period. A man of independent means thanks to his farm and wool business, he was the first Englishman to win both a continental Grand Prix and the Le Mans 24-hours. His racing career commenced before the war and he won the 1938 Australian GP, a handicap affair, with an ERA B-type. 'South of the equator' was subsequently to become a happy hunting ground for Whitehead, somewhere he could continue to win in events such as the 1953 Lady Wigram Trophy and the Rand GP. As well as racing his cars, he sold them to the locals, as he intended to do with 0578M in 1956.

Following action in the Royal Tank Corps during the war, Whitehead continued to campaign his now ageing ERA, finishing seventh in the 1947 French GP and second in the British Empire Trophy. He persuaded Ferrari to sell him a short chassis 125 F1 car in 1948. He used this patriotically painted green car to compete regularly throughout 1949 and then in many rounds of the first two years of the Formula One World Championship with a third place – three laps behind a couple of Alfa Romeos – in the 1950 French GP easily his best result. However, his win (one of three that year) in the 1949 Czech GP when the works Ferraris were absent was the first part of the double-header mentioned at the top. His achievements that year were recognised with the BRDC Gold Star.

Whitehead's greatest motor sport moment is victory in the 1951 Le Mans 24-hours, the first for a Jaguar. He and Peter Walker won by 19 laps, setting a new record speed despite enduring 16 hours of rain. He continued to compete in F1 and F2 races, although only a couple of World Championship meetings each year. He also drove for the Jaguar factory in both C- and D-types to win the 12 Hours of Hyères (with Tom Cole) and, twice, the 12 Hours of Reims (with, consecutively Stirling Moss and Ken Wharton). Whitehead's final two years at Le Mans were with Aston Martin, partnered by his half-brother Graham Whitehead. The pair finished second in 1958. In September that year they were sharing a Jaguar 3.4-litre on the Tour de France Automobile and were leading their class. Fog abounded as the event drew to a conclusion and Graham crashed over a bridge and into a ravine near Nimes. Peter was killed instantly.

● Peter Whitehead, seen here in 1951, competed at World Championship Grand Prix level with this green Ferrari 125.
Grand Prix Library

The other side of the world

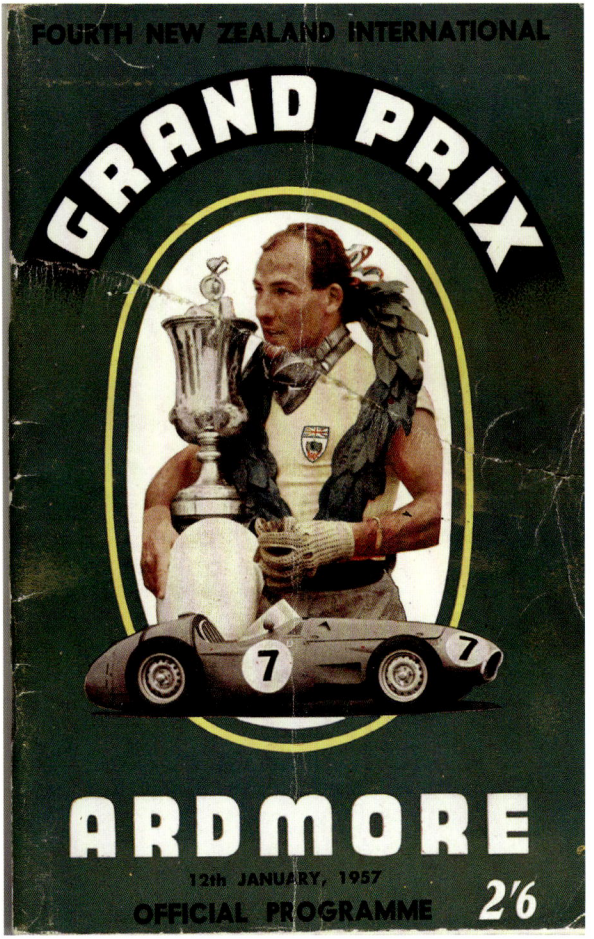

The programme cover for the 1957 New Zealand Grand Prix shows the previous year's winner, Stirling Moss and his Maserati 250F. The Englishman would not return to the race until 1960. Also missing from the entry list is a Ferrari 857S. Ross Jensen would not reveal his intention to race the car until after the programme had been printed and can be seen as entered in his Austin-Healey.
Courtesy Mark Holman

race he accordingly installed extra tankage behind the passenger compartment.

Jensen first heard of Wharton's death when he was on the starting grid. According to the March 1957 issue of Australian magazine *Wheels*: 'A story went around during the race that some stupid pit monkey had told Jensen that Wharton's earlier crash had been caused by some inherent defect in the Monza and Jensen had lost his nerve in consequence. He confounded such detractors by driving a magnificent race and finishing the first Kiwi home, in fourth slot.'

Local man Roy Roycroft led at first with his Ferrari 375 ahead of the Super Squalos of Whitehead and Reg Parnell and, initially, Ross Jensen, who was delighted to find himself keeping up with the single-seaters. 'I was staying with them on the opening lap,' he recalled.

However, the extra fuel tank had upset the fragile balance of the '0584M' and Jensen had not had time to test his modification on the track before the race. He fell back, finding himself in a duel for eighth place with the Cooper T41s of his unrelated namesake, Syd Jensen and Alex Stringer and the Jaguar XK120 of Bob Gibbons. Then, on the 10th lap, 'as we entered the Cloverleaf at the end of the back straight, the Monza didn't respond as required and it went straight on. I gathered it but it took the rest of the race to overcome the deficit. It's easy to outsmart oneself at times.'

Gibbons went past and it would be many laps before the Ferrari again headed the Jaguar. Retirements up ahead, including Roycroft who was suffering from heatstroke, meant that Ross could eventually move up to fourth place, winning the Leonard Lord Trophy and

The other side of the world

£150 for first New Zealander home as a result. Said the local press: 'The New Zealand drivers can congratulate themselves for their display this year. They did better than ever before. R. Jensen's fourth place is the highest that has ever been gained in the four Grands Prix by a New Zealander.'

Up-front, there were last minute dramas as Parnell's brakes failed and 0584M's owner Whitehead closed to within 2.6sec of his team-mate. Also ahead of Jensen at the end was Australian Stan Jones, father of future World Champion Alan, in a Maserati 250F.

19 January 1957, Levin, New Zealand
Car number unknown, Ross Jensen: **retired.**
The week after the NZ Grand Prix, Jensen was entered for a minor race meeting – the crowd was only 10,000, poor for those days – at Levin, winning the sports car race with his Austin-Healey but dropping out of the main event with 0584M due to a gearbox problem. Although this was a minor event, it was said that plans were already being made for an international race at Levin the following year that would fully establish the little Horowhenua circuit. (Jensen finished fourth the following year at the first Levin International, driving his Maserati 250F.)

26 January 1957, Lady Wigram Trophy, Wigram Aerodrome, Christchurch, New Zealand
Car number 8, Ross Jensen: **finished 4th.**
Ross and 0548M were out again the next weekend for the 150-mile Lady Wigram Trophy at the RNZAF Wigram airfield. Practice resulted in them being ninth fastest and on the third row of the grid for the race. Said The *Christchurch Star-Sun* newspaper after practice: 'Sports car drivers Ross Jensen and (Bob) Gibbons acquitted themselves well. Always steady and never spectacular, they kept well ahead of some cars which on paper looked considerably faster.'

In baking heat and before a crowd reportedly 25-35,000 strong, Ross was up to fifth place on the first lap, albeit well behind the leading quartet. Throughout the race he battled with his namesake Syd. The Ferrari had twice the engine capacity of the Climax-engined Cooper, and the extra power was obvious. It was observed that Ross seemed to manage the power and the tricky handling of 0548M well. He was later to drive a theoretically better handling Lister-Jaguar but he never seemed to control this as well as the Ferrari.

Syd was suffering from oil whipped up in front of his low Cooper, forcing him into the pit on a couple of occasions.

● In the wake of Ken Wharton's tragic accident, only one of the two Ferrari 'Monzas' expected - '0578M/0584M' - raced in New Zealand during 1956. *Stenberg Archive*

Ferrari 857S | 75

The other side of the world

Ross Jensen

Would New Zealander Ross Jensen have made it as a Grand Prix driver? We shall never know but there were those who thought he had the talent. He had been brought over to Europe to drive for the Lister-Jaguar sports cars team in 1958. Reg Parnell, who had competed against him in New Zealand, tried to persuade him to join BRM for the following season. 'He was a lot better driver than he appeared to be at Lister,' recalls future Grand Prix pilot and fellow New Zealander Howden Ganley, who observed much of his early career.

The 1959 season saw the marque score its first victory in a round of the World Championship (Joakim Bonnier in Holland). However, Ross and his wife Hazel had left their two children behind with their grandmother in NZ. Family and work ties were too strong and Jensen decided to return to his homeland. 'After some days of deliberating, I chose to favour my commercial interests in New Zealand as well as family responsibilities,' he later recalled. He also felt the other New Zealander then making his mark, Bruce McLaren, was then at the start of his career, 'where I was well into mine'.

That career had included a significant season with Ferrari 0578/0584M, a car which first gave him the opportunity to run competitively in NZ's major races. Growing up on a dairy farm in Auckland, Jensen first raced motorcycles prior to the Second World War. The hostilities over, he took to four wheels, initially with an Austin 7, and in 1951 set up his own motor business in Newmarket. That year he became Provincial Sedan Car Champion.

The first New Zealand Grand Prix in 1951 was a very local affair but the second, in 1954, attracted some foreign entries. Also on the grid was Jensen in one of the team of Austin-Healey 100/4 cars entered by Austin importer Seabrook-Fowlds. Ross finished seventh behind half-a-dozen pukka racing cars. He then bought his own Austin-Healey, a faster 100S, and his performance with it made him one of two New Zealanders invited to participate in the 1956 Australian Grand Prix. Here he first came to the attention of Peter Whitehead (see main text) and to his crucial season with 0578/0584M.

Single-seaters had to be the next important move and, for 1958, Ross Jensen acquired a Maserati 250F. This was not any old 250F but chassis 2508, the very car that arguably saved the flagging career of Stirling Moss.

● Jensen proved his worth in the UK during 1958 racing a Lister-Jaguar, fittingly winning the Scott-Brown Memorial Trophy at Snetterton. However, he declined to stay in Europe despite an offer to drive for BRM.
LAT Images

76 | Exceptional Cars

The other side of the world

Back in November 1953, Moss's father Alfred worried that his son's career was stalling; he sent Stirling's manager Ken Gregory on a last-minute trip to Italy to get his lad a factory drive. Arriving, weary, in the evening at Modena, Gregory decided to try Maserati. He was told there was no possibility of a works position for Stirling, but would he like to buy one of the new Maserati 250Fs? Gregory agreed and then had to ring 'Poppa' Moss to see how the car could be paid for. Meanwhile, Stirling himself was on the *Queen Mary* returning from a holiday in the Bahamas, and totally unaware of what was being done on his behalf.

The 250F proved Moss could be a front-running Grand Prix driver, soon leading to factory drives with Maserati and then Mercedes-Benz. Now repainted in grey, his 2508 continued to contest non-Championship races, but by the end of 1955 it had served its purpose and was sold, via Maserati, to Jensen for the 1958 season. In those days, the Italian government paid a bonus for exports, and Gregory recalled: '[Maserati] worked out that if they gave it a different chassis plate, which they did by putting one plate on top of the original, they would get a second bonus. This raised a serious problem later when [renowned journalist] Denis Jenkinson wrote a piece about Jensen being cheated out of the original Stirling Moss car by me. He had investigated and found it had a different chassis number. There was a libel incident, but whatever I got I gave to charity.'

Jensen quickly settled in with his 250F. He finished second in the New Zealand Grand Prix, the first 'local' home, and was beaten only by Jack Brabham's more modern, rear-engined Cooper-Climax. Jensen's first win came at Dunedin, a masterful performance that made him the first Kiwi to come first in a major race over class internationals on home soil. A week later he again beat compatriot Bruce McLaren (Cooper-Climax) in dominating the first Teretonga International. This time, third place was taken by Brabham who shortly after, of course, won the first of his three World Championships. The end of the season saw Ross again win the New Zealand Gold Star with over twice the number of points scored by McLaren. 'He was very quick in the 250F,' remembers Ganley. 'It suited his style.'

Archie Scott Brown, who raced against Ross that year, recommended him to Brian Lister, which resulted in a factory drive in England. He acquitted himself well, winning at Snetterton. When Scott Brown was killed at Spa-Francorchamps, Jensen's workload increased. His performances demonstrated his talent but he was not really happy in England, and returned to New Zealand.

There he purchased another, rebodied 250F, the 'Grey Lady' having been sold. The new car was painted blue and yellow and entered into races under the name of the fictitious 'Royal Santa Ana Automobile Club of El Salvador' for reasons that remain unclear. The NZ season proved mainly one of retirements, although there was a second place in the rain-curtailed Waimate 50. Over Easter the car was shipped to Australia for a Bathurst race. Not much was expected but by lap five Jensen was in the lead and remained there. This was despite the fact he was feeling unwell and went down with pneumonia the following day. The Maserati had to go, though, and Ross moved onto the New Zealand Touring Car Championship with a Jaguar. The ensuing Saloon Gold Star was his final major Championship win, and he subsequently retired from driving while remaining active in the NZ racing scene.

● The first time out in '0578M/0584M' for Jensen was at Ardmore. It was a great opportunity for the New Zealander.
Jim Barclay

The other side of the world

The first of these enabled Ross to move back into fifth place and remain ahead of his fellow Jensen. The race developed into something of a procession, although Ross moved up to an eventual fourth place when burly Maserati 250F driver Horace Gould stopped with heat exhaustion. At the finish he was two laps behind his car's owner Whitehead – after, said the local press, 'an armchair ride' – with Jack Brabham (Cooper-Climax) second and Roycroft (Ferrari) third. *Autosport* magazine reported that Jensen had 'a steady, unspectacular race'.

2 February 1957, Dunedin Road Race, Dunedin, New Zealand. *Car number 17, Ross Jensen:* **finished 4th**
Ross raced 0548M at six events that winter. At the rough and slow, round-the-houses and wharves track of Dunedin, he was quicker than the other Jensen in practice. His sixth place put him on the second row of the grid. Once more he was to finish fourth in the race, after another tussle with his namesake, three laps behind winner Parnell, who was followed home by Brabham and Whitehead. It was Reg's last victory as a driver after

● Chassis '0578M/0584M' in the paddock for the Lady Wigram Trophy. This photograph clearly shows the airfield nature of the Wigram circuit. *Terry Marshall Archives*

23 eventful seasons. The local press reported that Ross, who was again the first Kiwi home, was 'never really prominent, but came in fourth after a number of cars had been forced to retire.' The paper also listed him, and the Ferrari, as winning Class 3 of the Greg Anderson Memorial Race for Sports Cars the same day. However, Eoin Young reported that he was driving the Austin-Healey – which he was continuing to campaign with success that season – in this race. The overall winner was Jack Brabham's smaller Cooper 'Bobtail' behind which Ross, whatever car he was driving, finished second overall.

16 February 1957, New Zealand Championship Road Race, Ryal Bush, New Zealand
Car number 18, Ross Jensen: **finished 5th.**
Virtually the same field appeared at the rectangular and fast Ryal Bush road course a week later. Ross was moving up the grid and was in fourth spot on the second row for this New Zealand Championship Road Race – the narrowness of the track meant a 2-2-2 formation. The first lap was precarious, surprise pole sitter, Horace Gould (Maserati 250F) botching the start. But it saw Ross well back in 12th place having spun on the third bend with grabbing brakes. By the end of the 27-lap contest, he was up to fifth, despite the brakes continuing to malfunction. Having been the first Kiwi home at Ardmore, second at Dunedin, and now second local again to Roycroft at Ryal Bush, he was looking favourite for the inaugural New Zealand Gold Star, which was modelled on the British Racing Drivers' Club's similarly-named competition (points were awarded on a results per race basis, just as for its older British counterpart). Up front, Whitehead, himself the winner of the 1949 BRDC Gold Star, won again, the last victory of his career.

21 February 1957, South Island Championship Road Race, Mairehau, New Zealand
Car number 18, Ross Jensen: **Finished 5th, also 4th in the All-Comers Race and 2nd in the Sports Car Race.**
Another week, another track. This time it was Mairehau, and the very last time this circuit would be used. Many of the overseas drivers had returned home, which gave a very different look to the entry. A number of the cars had, though, been acquired by locals, and Ross Jensen still had Whitehead's 750 Monza for his final race with the car.

Just before the event, billed in long-winded fashion as the Christchurch Festival Road Race and South Island Championship Road Race, Whitehead was seen wishing Tom Clark, who had acquired his Super Squalo, good fortune. He then moved on to Ross to do the same. This was arguably Jensen and the Ferrari's best chance of success and, at the end of the first lap, Ross was in third place. However, he was observed by *The Press* newspaper to be working hard to keep 'the big sports car at top speed round the corners.'

Just behind the Ferrari, the old Maserati 8CLT of Frank Shuter seemed to oil up a couple of plugs on the pit bend before, 'with several splutters', accelerating along the following straight. As the *Star-Sun* reported, making 'his big bid' he then shot past Ross and into third. Gradually overhauling them was John McMillan who was now beginning to get the hang of his ex-Parnell Super Squalo. On the 18th lap he was past Jensen, taking Shuter one circuit later. Ross finished only in fifth. Jensen and the Ferrari were particularly busy that day, coming fourth in the 25-mile All-Comers Race, which was also won by Clark and second in the 15-mile Sports Car Race, beaten by June Monk's Triumph TR2. Both events were decided on handicap with Mrs Monk, who drove 'brilliantly' according to *The Press*, also finishing second in the All-Comers contest ahead of both Jensens.

Despite only finishing fifth in the main event, with his main rival for the title Roycroft absent, Ross Jensen was assured of the Gold Star with 35 points. Chassis 0578M (or should that be 0584M?) took its driver to a significant title. However, Whitehead was unable to find a buyer for it in New Zealand and it was returned to the factory. Quite when this happened is open to question. Author David McKinney reported it was still in Auckland in June 1957, but historian Antoine Prunet points out its steering box is stamped '3.5.57'.

● The 'sister' of '0578M/0584M', the car that Ken Wharton had lost his life in, 0514M, remains in New Zealand and is now in the Southward Museum, near Wellington. It was beautifully restored with a new aluminium body, by Ken Harris who raced it in the 1958, 1959 and 1960 New Zealand Grands Prix, as well as elsewhere.
Terry Marshall Archives

Chapter 7
Viking saga

The racing career of 0578M can be divided into three distinct time periods: its career as a factory car; its time 'Down Under'; and, finally, its adventures in Scandinavia. It seems that '0584M', as the car was still being referred to, having returned from New Zealand, remained in Italy until late 1958.

The season before Olle Persson crashed badly the Ferrari Svezia-entered 750 Monza that he was to have shared with rally legend Erik Carlsson in practice for the Swedish Grand Prix – that year, it was a round of the World Sportscar Championship. Carlsson then teamed up with the damaged car's owner John Kvarnström to finish seventh in another 750 Monza.

Kvarnström subsequently visited the Ferrari factory with the Swedish marque importer Tore Bjurström, and purchased 0578M/0584M minus its engine. The void under the bonnet was instantly filled with the 3-litre unit from the now unusable car crashed by Persson at Kristianstad. Historian Antoine Prunet points out that the invoice from the purchase, referenced 979/58, is undated in the certificate of origin, but that an invoice from *Scuderia* Ferrari dated 10 October 1958 places the sale in the last two months of that year.

10 May 1959 Eläintarhanajo, Helsinki, Finland
Car number 14, John Kvarnström: **finished 4th.**
The first Scandinavian race for the car, which was listed in the entry as an 857S, was the 1959 Eläintarhanajo at Helsinki, Finland's equivalent to a Grand Prix meeting and a city circuit event that Kvarnström had won three years previously with his 750 Monza (chassis 0470MD). The meeting was now coming of age, this being its 21st running. On the racecard were motorcycles, 500cc single-seaters, GTs and sports cars under and over 2-litre, the latter of 25 laps on a track made treacherous by oil and rubber left from the previous races. Added to that, the tar had begun to melt, even in practice.

Around 80,000 paying customers lined the 2km track adjacent to the Olympic Stadium which could be accurately described as a true road circuit. The narrow track – the cars could only line up two-by-two on the grid – was in a picturesque woodland setting. In fact, the trees were so close that there was no margin for error, as Andre Pilette discovered to his cost in practice, completely wrecking the Ecurie Belge Lister-Jaguar while, fortunately, walking away unscathed himself.

Kvarnström finished fourth in the main event (and third in the over 2-litre class), the second Ferrari home, the winner having been an inspired Carl-Otto Bremer in his 750 Monza. Second was former 0578M owner Peter Whitehead (Aston Martin DBR1), who enjoyed a shortlived lead at the start. Considerable work apparently was needed to make 0578M race-worthy for this contest. Bjurström's mechanic Rune Bertilsson told historian Tom Karlsson that the still-red car 'looked like it had been lying at the bottom of the sea'.

9 August 1959, Kanonloppet, Karlskoga, Sweden
Car number 15, John Kvarnström: **finished 7th.**
Three months later Kvarnström and the 857S were up against sterner stuff. A trio of that year's World Championship Grand Prix winners were on the grid for the annual Kanonloppet meet run on the outskirts of

● (Below) The 1959 Kanonloppet was not the first time that 0578M found itself up against cars driven by Stirling Moss and Jack Brabham. Both entered this time in Cooper Monacos, they were on the front row of the grid with Sweden's own Joakim Bonnier (Porsche). Starting further back on the grid, '0578M/0584M' would finish a lap adrift.
Örebro city archive

John Kvanström in '0578M/0584M' follows in the wake of Jack Brabham (Cooper-Climax T49) and Carl-Otto Bremer (Ferrari 750 Monza) at the Kanonloppet in 1959.
Örebro city archive

Viking saga

● The start of the 1960 Kanonloppet with Stirling Moss at the head of the field in one of the Lotus 19s that the British Racing Partnership had just acquired. It was Sir Stirling's first outing in what he would later say was 'one of my favourite cars'. A dark suited Kvanström runs to '0578M/0584M, which is third on the grid.
Örebro city archive

Karlskoga. Stirling Moss and the man who was to win his first World Championship title that year, Jack Brabham, both had Cooper Monaco T49s, while Joakim Bonnier was present with a Porsche 718 RSK. Moss was reported to be in a class of his own. He later described his win as 'not a bad result'. According to his diary, his car suffered from 'bad brakes, jumping [out of] second gear, duff clutch [and] broken roll bar connector', so perhaps he had a point. Anyway, as he said: 'I won a great big BP cup.'

Jack Brabham, with a smaller Coventry-Climax engine in his Cooper, finished second overall while winning the under 2-litre class. A problem with transporting Brabham's car to the track meant he almost missed the race, but the organisers were not going to lose out on such a star attraction so easily, and so rented a furniture truck to pick up both Brabham and his Cooper.

Seventh (and fifth in class) came Kvarnström, one lap behind the likes of Moss and Brabham.

15 August 1959, Copenhagen Grand Prix, Roskilde Ring, Copenhagen, Denmark
Car number 3, John Kvarnström: **finished 5th.**
A week late, Kvarnström and the Ferrari were in Denmark for the Copenhagen Grand Prix at the curvaceous Roskilde

82 | Exceptional Cars

Ring. This was a curious affair with two heats of 12 laps and two of 16 spread out over two days. Moss was again present with his own Cooper Monaco prepared by Mike Keele, the man behind Keele karts. By winning all four heats, Stirling took overall victory having, as he later wrote, 'put on a bit of a show racing against Jack Brabham's similar car [which finished third] and [second placed] David Piper's Lotus [15]'. Kvarnström was fifth and last of the small entry.

7 August 1960, Kanonloppet, Karlskoga, Sweden
Car number 15, John Kvarnström: **retired.**

A year later, many of the same names returned to Karlskoga for that year's Kanonloppet. Moss, Piper and Bonnier were all on the starting grid, along with Graham Whitehead, brother of 0578M's previous owner Peter. Back too was Kvarnström in said 857S. Moss had been hospitalised following a serious crash in the Belgian Grand Prix at Spa in June. After a rigorous programme of physiotherapy, he was ready to race again on 7 August, this time in one of the Lotus 19s newly acquired for the Yeoman Credit-backed British Racing Partnership. Once again, Moss was victorious, this time following what he described as 'a dice' with Bonnier's Camoradi

● Moss, unusually for him, may not have been the first to his car but he, nevertheless, hit the head of the field immediately. From the left, the grid lined up: Moss (Lotus 19), David Piper (Lotus 15), Kvanström in '0578M/0584M', Graham Whitehead (Lola Mk.1), Bo Ljungfeldt (Maserati 200S), Curt Lincoln (Cooper T49) and Jo Bonnier (Maserati Tipo 61).
Örebro city archive

Viking saga

Chassis '0578M/0584M' stayed on in Scandinavia, returning to the Kanonloppet meeting in 1966. Its attractive lines had, temporarily, been destroyed, and even if they were the Swedish national colours, it just did not look right in its new blue and yellow livery. *Current owner's archives*

USA-entered Maserati Tipo 61. Stirling reckoned this was the first day he used a bubble visor because of the rainy conditions. Star driver of the race was said to be Piper, following a comeback and an eventful time in his Lotus 15.

For Kvarnström it would be the worst result of his short partnership with 0578M/0584M because he retired – having been a contender for a couple of laps – with a broken rear axle after six of the 25 circuits. It was his last race with the car.

The next we hear of it is in 1963, when it was registered in Stockholm by Ake Jansson. It had lost the graceful lines of its youth, having been fitted with 6.5in wide Borrani wheels which have dictated flared, bloated wings. In February 1966 Jansson advertised the car in *Road & Track* magazine, offering it for sale for a 'best offer over US$2000'. It remained in Scandinavia, however, being purchased by young enthusiast Björn Bellander from Gustavsberg near Stockholm. Bellander recalled borrowing SKR3000 from his mother-in-law and also throwing in a Morris Minor to pay for it. Prior to his purchase, the Ferrari had been involved in an accident on the public road with an Opel Kapitan. Major surgery had to be carried out on the front end on the right, the windscreen and the transmission, the work being carried out in an old grocery store. It was a long way from the Ferrari factory. Other work included reassembling the engine and fitting a new Nardi steering wheel. Bellander could not later remember if the original had been with the car when he bought it. He also decided to paint it in Swedish national colours, dark blue with white and yellow central stripes.

21 August 1966, Kanonloppet, Karlskoga, Sweden
Car number 21, Björn Bellander: **finished 2nd.**
It was back to Karlskoga for the historic race at the 1966 Kanonloppet. Bellander later recalled: 'We were wonderfully ignorant of what opponents we had from England …without having any experience of our cars before. It was a wonderful day and we walked around in a wonderful rush of happiness among Maseratis, ERAs, Bugattis and other celebrity car brands. It would be a fantastic race.'

Bellander performed well, finishing practice in third place despite claiming not to 'take time training so seriously'. He was told to take it easy at the beginning. However, he then probably over-revved a little at the start and was quickly overtaken by a number of other cars. Still, he hauled himself back into contention and finished second for which he eventually received the prize of a pair of silver candlesticks.

In July two years later, Bellander advertised the car, which he then referred to as an 850 Monza, in *Autosport*:

The car was also advertised in *Road & Track* with the emphasis placed on the blue paint and the 'specially ordered Borranis'. There was an early response and the

John Kvarnström

John Kvarnström raced as an amateur throughout the 1950s and was one of the leading Swedish drivers of his day. He owned two Ferrari 750 Monzas, the first having been purchased from Gunnar Carlsson. His debut race with this, the 1956 Eläintarhanajo, Finland's most important race, resulted in pole position and victory, just over 5sec ahead of Carlsson in a similar car. This was followed by fourth place in the Swedish Grand Prix partnered by Erik Lundgren, the pair entered by Swedish Ferrari importer Tore Bjurström. They were also first in the over 2-litre class, but five laps behind the overall winner.

However, unlike the Eläintarhanajo, the Sveriges GP was notably a round of the World Sportscar Championship and the three cars ahead of them were all *Scuderia* Ferrari factory machines, headed by the 290MM of Phil Hill and Maurice Trintignant, both future drivers of 0578M. Kvarnström's third race of the year with his first 750 Monza was the Kanonloppet at Karlskoga. Three such cars were on the entry list, Kvarnström finishing third behind those of Carlsson and another future 0578M competitior, Alfonso de Portago.

The following year Kvarnström completed only one lap at the Eläintarhanajo before retiring with an engine malady. At Kiruna he finished fourth behind three other Ferraris, two of them 750 Monzas, and then came the Swedish Grand Prix in practice for which, as recounted in this chapter, his 750 Monza was badly damaged and resulted in the purchase of 0578M or '0584M' as it was then known. He continued to campaign the car until 1960, his last year as a serious racing driver, although he was seen in rallying as late as 1966.

The gentle Kvarnström, whose driving style was described as 'very smooth', started racing with a Plymouth just after the Second World War. This was replaced by his own, home-built Hudson-based special which he first campaigned at the Eläintarhanajo, finishing fourth in 1950 and third the year after. Commanding his Hudson, once memorably described as 'hideous', Kvarnström became one of the leading lights in the Nordic special class on ice and gravel. That Hudson Special was eventually replaced by an Allard, and then a Ford-based special. His first important event was the 1955 Swedish Grand Prix, a non-Championship event that year but one with a stellar, if small, cast including eventual first and second, Juan Manuel Fangio and Stirling Moss in their Mercedes-Benz 300SLRs. Kvarnström was entered in an Alfa Romeo 6C 3000 by future Grand Prix driver Joakim Bonnier but was the sole retirement during the 32-lap race. That season was his first with a Ferrari, finishing second in the Kanonloppet Production GT over-2-litre race with a 250MM. From the beginning of the following season, he remained loyal to the Ferrari marque until the end of his racing career.

● John Kvanström (left) in company with Tore Bjurström (centre) and Enzo Ferrari, himself (right). *Tony Ring archives*

Viking saga

Viking saga

(Right) Chassis 0578M sitting (far right) in the paddock at Karlskoga in 1966.
Current owner's archives

(Left) A Scandinavian trio: John Kvanström in '0578M/0584M' trails Bo Ljunfeltdt (Maserati 200S) and Curt Lincoln (Cooper T49) during the 1960 Kanonloppet.
Örebro city archive

(Above) Stirling Moss would later recall that the 1960 Kanonloppet was the first time that he 'used a helmet with a "bubble" visor in rainy conditions'
Örebro city archive

(Right) Unwilling to be in hospital for a moment longer than was necessary, Stirling Moss set off for Sweden just six weeks after a massive accident at Spa-Francorchamps. As he later stated, 'I celebrated my return to the cockpit by winning after a dice with Jo Bonnier's Maserati.'
Örebro city archive

Ferrari 857S

Viking saga

car sold to dealer Dan Margulies in London for £1,000; according to Bellander, the car was 'loaded on to a boat on 24 August 1968'. As he wrote: 'How could I?' On the bill of lading between Bellander and Margulies, the Ferrari is described as 'one used motorcar'.

Margulies quickly found a customer for '0584M', as it was still known, in Wolf Zeuner who road-registered it as WOY 8G. From Zeuner it passed into the hands of Channel Islander Angus Spencer-Nairn in 1979. On March 1 it was re-registered in Jersey as J 9060 in order to compete in historic rallies. More importantly, Spencer-Nairn got rid of the un-Ferrari-like blue, white and yellow livery and repainted it Italian red. He also changed the wheels and removed those flared wings so that 0578M/0584M was looking its old self again.

An inspection in the mid-1990s by Antoine Prunet confirmed that what Spencer-Nairn had purchased was, indeed, 0578M and not 0584M, the chassis number under which it had masqueraded since being sold to Whitehead nearly 40 years before. Prunet also found that the 3-litre engine Kvarnström had taken from his earlier 750 Monza (0470MD) was still in place.

The number '0584M' was stamped on a small square plaque welded on the front crossmember of square section. Nowhere on the chassis itself was there any other indication that this was the number of the car. What also made Prunet suspicious was the welded plate, which was not Ferrari's usual practice of attachment. He therefore asked Spencer-Nairn if he would mind having the plate removed to see what was underneath it. Prunet was not present when the work was carried out but was pleased to eventually receive a letter stating, 'as predicted by you chassis number 0578M was revealed!' The stamping was not on the horizontal face of the square tube but on the vertical front face. The fact that Spencer-Nairn's car was the original 0578M was underlined when it was noticed that the identity 54DSN on the gearbox casing matched that on 0578M's assembly forms.

In theory, that should have been that as to the car's identity. However, the original 0584M was still around. This turned up as Lot 93 at Coys' Silverstone auction in July 1987. Confusion still surrounded it. The catalogue stated that it was '0578M' but listed a totally different race history - including Peter Collins's win on the Giro di Sicilia - to that recorded in this book. Graham Earl, who had prepared the catalogue, recalls how he was surprised to receive a telephone call from Spencer-Nairn, pointing out that he owned the real 0578M. He was able to convince Earl that the car Coys was selling was 0584M, but it was too late to reprint before the auction.

The genuine 0578M also went to auction in December 2000, still being referred to as '0584M (ex-0578M)'. Also offered for sale at the same Bonhams & Brooks auction in Gstaad was a 3.5-litre Tipo 129 engine, described in the catalogue as stamped 0578M with internal number '129 N4'. Prolific car collector, Dutchman Evert Louwman, the seller and also a shareholder in Bonhams and Brooks, was said to have acquired it from the late Nigel Moores's collection. It was thought that during 1960 it had seen service powering the Cooper Monaco of JBW constructor Brian Naylor. The car failed to sell but immediately after the auction Spencer-Nairn purchased the 3.5-litre engine. It was then installed into 0578M by highly respected engineers Hall and Hall. Chassis 0578M was back to being a true Ferrari 857S, restored to the state it was that day in January 1956 when it finished second in a World Sportscar Championship round. In 2003, Hall and Hall sold the car for Spencer-Nairn and it moved to North America, where it competed in the Group 3A category at the 2004 Monterey Historic Automobile Races at Laguna Seca, where Ferrari was that year's featured marque. Still, though, it was being referred to as '0584M', despite Prunet's revelation.

● In 1979, 0578M was registered in Jersey and repainted in Italian red. *Hall & Hall*

● Seen on Laguna Seca's famed corkscrew section, 0578M competed in the Monterey Historic Automobile Races in 2004.
Martin Spetz

Part 3
A Fitting Tribute

The Mille Miglia was the epitome of road racing, one thousand miles of full-on competition around Italian towns and countryside and tackled in anything from a Fiat 500 to a V12 Ferrari. The year 1955 was surely one of the most memorable ever. Invariably an Italian, familiar with the open roads of his native land, in an Italian car, would win the race. That year, though, saw a young Englishman, guided by his bearded journalist compatriot, take a German car to victory in one of the greatest sporting achievements of the century.

Until 1954, Ferrari had won the Mille Miglia for six consecutive years. Then Alberto Ascari finished first in his Lancia D24. Now Ferrari was faced by a new challenge – the Mercedes-Benz 300SLRs – one of which was to be driven by Stirling Moss with Denis Jenkinson at his side. Ferrari's four-cylinder cars were still not regarded as the weapon of choice for World Championship rounds, and the factory entered a trio of V6 3.7-litre 118LMs for Umberto Maglioli, Paolo Marzotto and Piero Taruffi. Eugenio Castellotti had one of the new 4.4-litre 121LMs. Nine four-cylinder Ferraris did also start, five of them 750 Monzas, but all apart from that of Sergio Sighinolfi were privately entered. Two of these, both of whom drove 0578M during 1955, finished in the top six: Maglioli in third and Sighinolfi sixth. One has to assume that 0578M itself languished that weekend back in Maranello, its World Championship career yet to start.

Fast forward to 2016; 0578M is at Brescia, about to start its first retrospective Mille Miglia in the hands of its new owner.

The province of Brescia is steeped in motor sport history having hosted the Brescia Speed Weeks before the Great War and the first Italian Grand Prix in 1921. Its capital has seen the start of every Mille Miglia since the first in 1927 and remains its host to this day. Thus 0578M (308) is seen here in a fitting setting.
Current owner's archives

Chapter 8
Modern Times

The original Mille Miglia race was, as recounted earlier, brought to a close following the tragic occurrences of 1957. Twenty years later it was 'reborn' as a regularity event for cars of the type that would have been eligible to contest the races from 1927 onwards. Although Ferrari 857S 0578M did not take part in the 1950s, the criteria for the modern event stipulate that only the model has to have participated in period. Due to the fact that five 750 Monzas contested the 1955 race, 0578M is eligible to compete in the modern-day event. Although failing to get past Rome on its first contemporary appearance in 2016, 0578M has twice more appeared on the Mille Miglia.

In 2014, 0578M left North America for Europe via the UK before arriving in Maranello, accompanied by Ferrari historian Antoine Prunet and with all the requisite documentation that established the provenance of the car. It then remained at Ferrari for most of 2015.

The situation with Ferrari's classic car department, *Ferrari Classiche*, is that when certifying *any* car, it also has to 'put it right' in-house with original parts, and it was now time for 0578M to begin the process. It was clear that cosmetic work still needed to be done, not least because Ferrari required that it appeared as it was at a specific, period race and the 1956 Sebring 12-hours configuration was decided upon. This involved bringing the car back to where it should have been forward of the headlights: at some point, there had been a front-end accident. Also in period, small round vents had been cut in under the headlights. There was also some tidying up around the wheel arches, which had been modified in Sweden, the seats needed to be re-upholstered and the car was repainted in the correct shade of red. It was not a ground-up restoration, as is often the case: the car was in pretty good condition with its complete, original body. It should also be pointed out that it is not only the bodywork that is original: 0578M still features the original chassis and all mechanical components, a factor that is extremely rare in a racing car of its age.

The immediate ambition was to get the car ready for the Mille Miglia in May 2016, which involved an aggressive schedule and meant that the certification process was incomplete when the car headed off for the event. As the car appeared to function adequately, it was decided there was neither need nor time to address anything mechanical. The car was deemed ready but upon entering Rome there were some unusual noises coming from the engine bay. Continuing the event was certainly an option but one with potentially dire consequences. The car had not technically broken down, but at the makeshift workshop in the hotel parking area, it was discovered that the clearance in one of the valves had opened up significantly, and the car was officially retired.

After the Mille Miglia the car was returned to Ferrari. In early 2017 the car was sent to Ferrari specialist Philippe Rochat in Lausanne in preparation for the 2018 Mille Miglia, which it was to complete successfully. By now it had become apparent that the engine and gearbox needed more significant intervention, necessitating more specialist operations. Hall and Hall, which is renowned for its particular expertise with these four-cylinder engines received the power unit at its company base in Bourne, Lincolnshire. At the time, it was not known that Rick Hall's team had worked

● Umberto Maglioli drove 0578M on a number of occasions in 1955 but, for that year's Mille Miglia, he was at the wheel of a Scaglietti-bodied Ferrari 118LM. He finished third, in the first Italian car home.
Getty Images/Klemantaski Collection

● The medieval, 25-sided Fontana Maggiore in Perugia provides a temporary backdrop to 0578M's progress through Northern Italy.
Current owner's archives

92 | Exceptional Cars

Modern Times

● Only the nature of the number roundel gives away the fact 0578M is not back on the Italian roads of 1955.
Current owner's archives

Under the bonnet

In 1977 Rick Hall and Rob Fowler left BRM to form historic race car specialists Hall and Fowler. Fowler parted in 1998, after which Rick's son Rob became a partner in what is now known as Hall and Hall. As Hall and Fowler, one of the first power units they became involved with were the 2.5-litre BRM P25 4-cylinder engines, which have steel screw-in cylinder liners with a very fine thread sealing on laminated stainless steel sealing rings. These units are complex and very powerful but had a tendency towards problems for the piston due to liner distortion from being torqued in at approximately 900ft lb. However, Hall and Fowler eventually perfected the fitting and machining from cast iron.

'The 4-cylinder Ferrari's engine had a similar design and suffered the same problems,' says Rick, 'We were being asked to rebuild these as well, as they also have screw-in liners with a coarse thread but seal on a taperseat. This is the Achilles heel of the engine, as is the camshaft and valve gear.

'We eventually rectified these problems and began making new parts, starting with crankcases as most were beyond service. Eventually we were able to manufacture complete new engines for all the Ferrari 4-cylinder range which includes 500 Mondial, 500 TR, 500 TRC, 625, 857 and 860.'

As recorded in the previous chapter, the company worked on the 3.0-litre 750 Monza engine that was previously fitted to chassis 0578M when owned by Angus Spencer-Nairn. In late 2000 when the car was still in his possession, the original 3.5-litre 857S power unit became available, with some damage and certain parts missing. Hall and Hall completely rebuilt this and fitted it to the car, selling the 750 Monza engine that was taken out.

'In 2017 the current owner asked if we could take a look at the engine as it was suffering from camshaft and cam follower troubles, another problematic area with these engines having very narrow camshaft lobes running on a steel roller fitted into the aluminium cam followers,' continues Hall. 'We rebuilt parts of the 857 engine and incorporated some of the valve gear modifications that we have completed over the years involving modern materials and metal treatments.'

Since the work, the car has competed in several events including the two Mille Miglias during which the engine has proven to be very reliable and run trouble free. 'It has been really great to be reacquainted with this great and rare engine, which we have worked on and known for over 30 years,' concludes Hall.

● The 3.5-litre four-cylinder engine, now restored to 0578M, seen on the workshop floor at Hall and Hall.
Hall and Hall

Modern Times

earlier on the same engine. It then stayed at Hall and Hall for the best part of 2017 (see side bar).

During this period, finer detailing of the bodywork and interior was carried out and more obscure, period parts such as the correct washer bottles and switches were sourced. In addition, the benign grey paint finish of the chassis was put right to the correct, original tone and matt finish that was still present in places. This is a detail that is often wrong, as it was never designed to be a decorative finish.

Simultaneously, the gearbox was sent to Pearsons Engineering in Roade, Northamptonshire, Gary Pearson having been recommended by Rick Hall. Pearsons had been responsible for looking after a 750 Monza 0568M, known as 'The Ice Racer' because of its competition experiences in Scandinavia. 'The ratios on "The Ice Racer" were particularly close: between fourth and fifth there were only a couple of rpm,' remembers Pearson. 'We changed third, fourth and fifth gears, as well as fitting taller final drives in the box. That lifted fifth gear

(Right) Chassis 0578M was sent to *Ferrari Classiche* for certification and, during this time, the factory took the opportunity to exhibit the car.
Currrent owner's archives

(Below) Day one of the 2019 Mille Miglia took 0578M past the 13th century Scaligero Caste in Sirmione.
Current owner's archives

96 | Exceptional Cars

Modern Times

● The Ferrari is not far from its Modenese homeland as it sweeps through Bologna's city centre.
Current owner's archives

[and] this all made the box a lot more useable.' On the back of this, Pearsons worked on another five 'Monza boxes', including that of 857S 0578M, reverting to its original configuration. 'It was a very useable "mod",' says Pearson. 'If people use these cars on the road in such events as the Mille Miglia, as they are increasingly doing instead of racing due to the value, then the ratios are a lot more suitable. As the box comes with a tall first gear, it is quite a close ratio unit, so if we had simply raised the final drive the first and second gears would have been way too tall, certainly for traffic. The difference afterwards is just vast.'

All this work, inevitably, took the better part of a year, precluding entry in any event until the engine and gearbox were reunited with the car. It was a rush to get the Ferrari back together for the 2018 Mille Miglia, in which the car ran flawlessly.

The Mille Miglia is renowned for its range of climatic conditions and often the event features rain in Brescia, a notoriously wet city by Italian standards especially at the beginning of the event. That year the rain was biblical. The current owner points out that the Ferrari 857S is of course, 'a *barchetta* and although, paradoxically, one does not notice the rain when you are on the move, when lining up at the start line in a queue of a few hundred cars you really do get wet. The answer is to have the largest umbrella that folds into the smallest possible package. Despite this inconvenience the car itself loves the rain as it keeps everything cool.' That was good as in 2018, it rained almost all the way around the course.

Experiencing a wide array of weather from snow to baking sunshine means there are frequently occasions when competitors have to take extra care and, in the case of 0578M, this is not made any easier by the fact that it is now fitted with modern Blockley tyres. They definitely look good, although the car should really be fitted with Engelbert tyres, which are no longer available.

The car finished the Mille Miglia with only a couple of minor problems: one of the headlights was no longer working and there had been trouble with the brakes. This related to the way in which the brake cables bifurcate next to the connection with the rear drums and their proximity to the suspension. This was a rudimentary problem but one that was causing the brake fluid to leak. Due to this, time was lost on the Friday evening returning from Rome. One of the benefits of breaking down, reckons the current custodian, is that 'it is enjoyable to see all the other remaining cars drive past.'

By the time 0578M had gained entry in the 2019 event, most of the niggling problems had been resolved. 'It generally takes years to sort a car out and get it running in a way that you want. I have never been able to do it in less than three years,' says the current owner.

There seems to be no doubt that Ferrari 857S 0578M has become a car to be used, be it on the way to the pub following a trip around the Cotswolds, motoring down the Great Glen or braving everything the Mille Miglia has to throw at it. Umberto Maglioli and Eugenio Castellotti would surely have approved.

● (Below) The starting ramp in Brescia for the Mille Miglia and 0578M is ready to return to the roads of Northern Italy.
Current owner's archives

● (Right) Ferrari 857S 0578M passing through Parma in the rain. In 2018, it poured almost all the way round the course of the Mille Miglia.
Current owner's archives

Modern Times

Ferrari 857S

Chapter 9
Photo gallery

Photography by Alex Howe

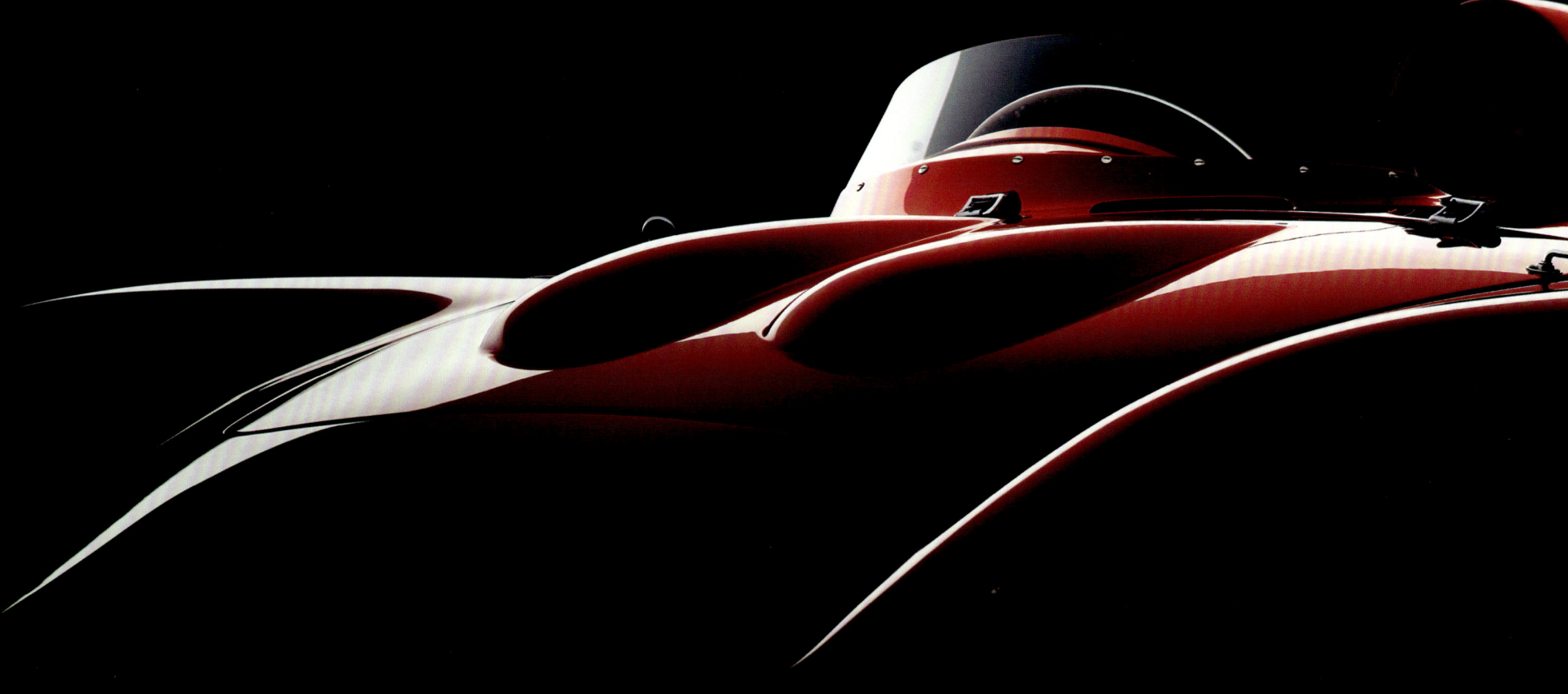

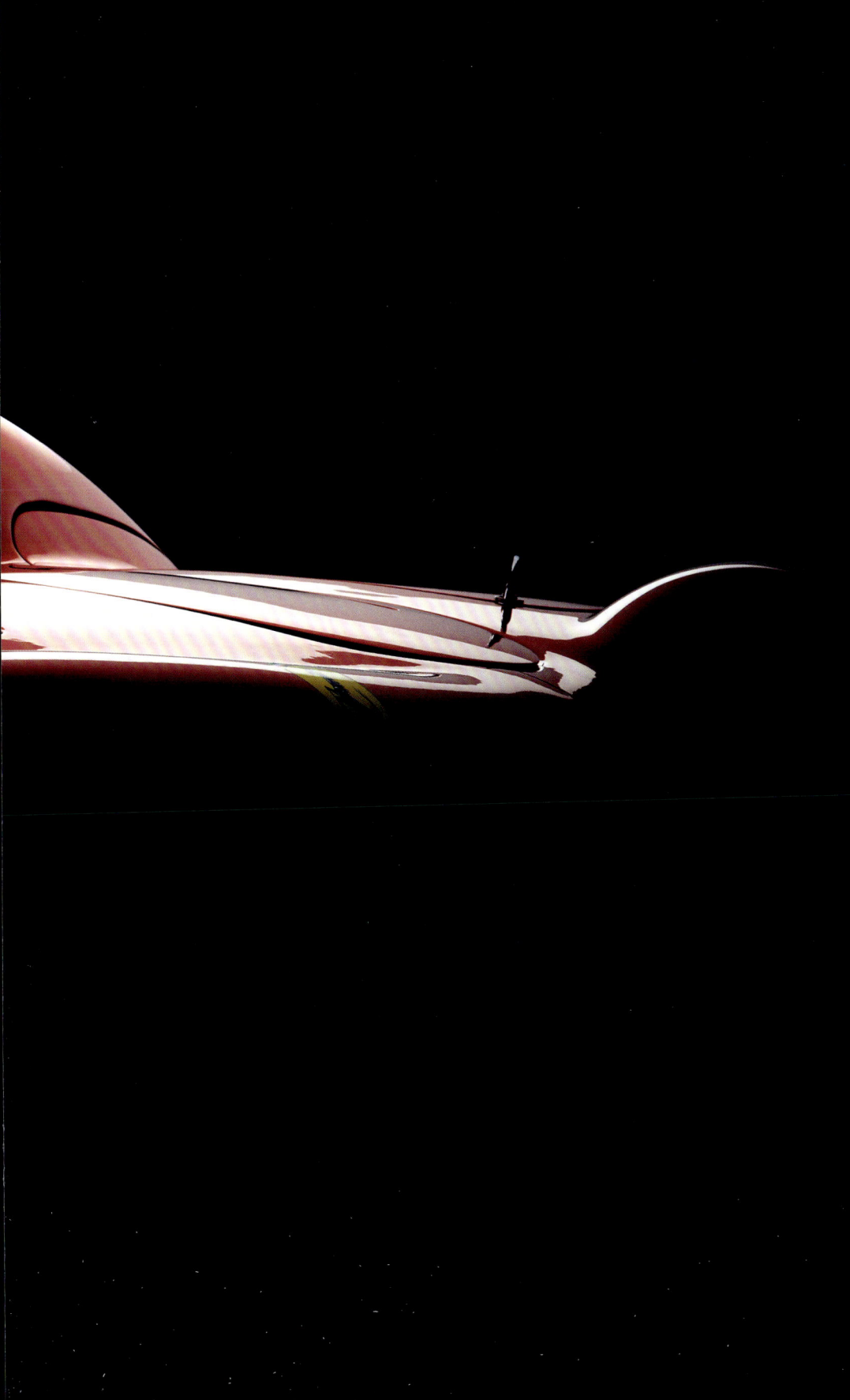

Ferrari chassis 0578M, like all the 857s, evolved during its early factory years as a race car. From the smooth lines of a 750 Monza to the arguably more purposeful and muscular body of an 857S, through a change of national identity from Italian red to a Swedish blue livery and on to attempts to recreate its earlier style, 0578M has, like most racing cars of the era, been through various iterations. With its present owner, who has a true feel for its heritage, the car is, as arguably it should be, exactly as it was when the factory ran her as a 3.5-litre contender.

The Ferrari 857S, and many of its type, straddle the boundary between racing and road car as, after all, many of the races were, like the Mille Miglia, on roads. Thus, it has all the attributes of a purposeful, if somewhat highly strung, road car but without any of the superfluous 'accessories' like soft tops and bumper bars, which, from a purist point of view, visually detract from the lines of many road cars.

The following photos illustrate and underline an era when, in a 1950's Ferrari, form really did meet function.

● It is perhaps true to say the Ferraris of the 1950's were, with the exception of their incredible engines, simply built to win races. The chassis and the bodies were just a canvas for the power units.

The 1950s were an incredible moment in time for the design world in Italy. There was a tremendous breadth of talent. Whether it be Scaglietti, Michelotti, Gandini, Giugiaro or Bertone, their names roll off the tongue. When you tasked a design studio like Scaglietti with skinning a car, such as the Ferrari 857S, and making it look good, you had nothing to worry about.

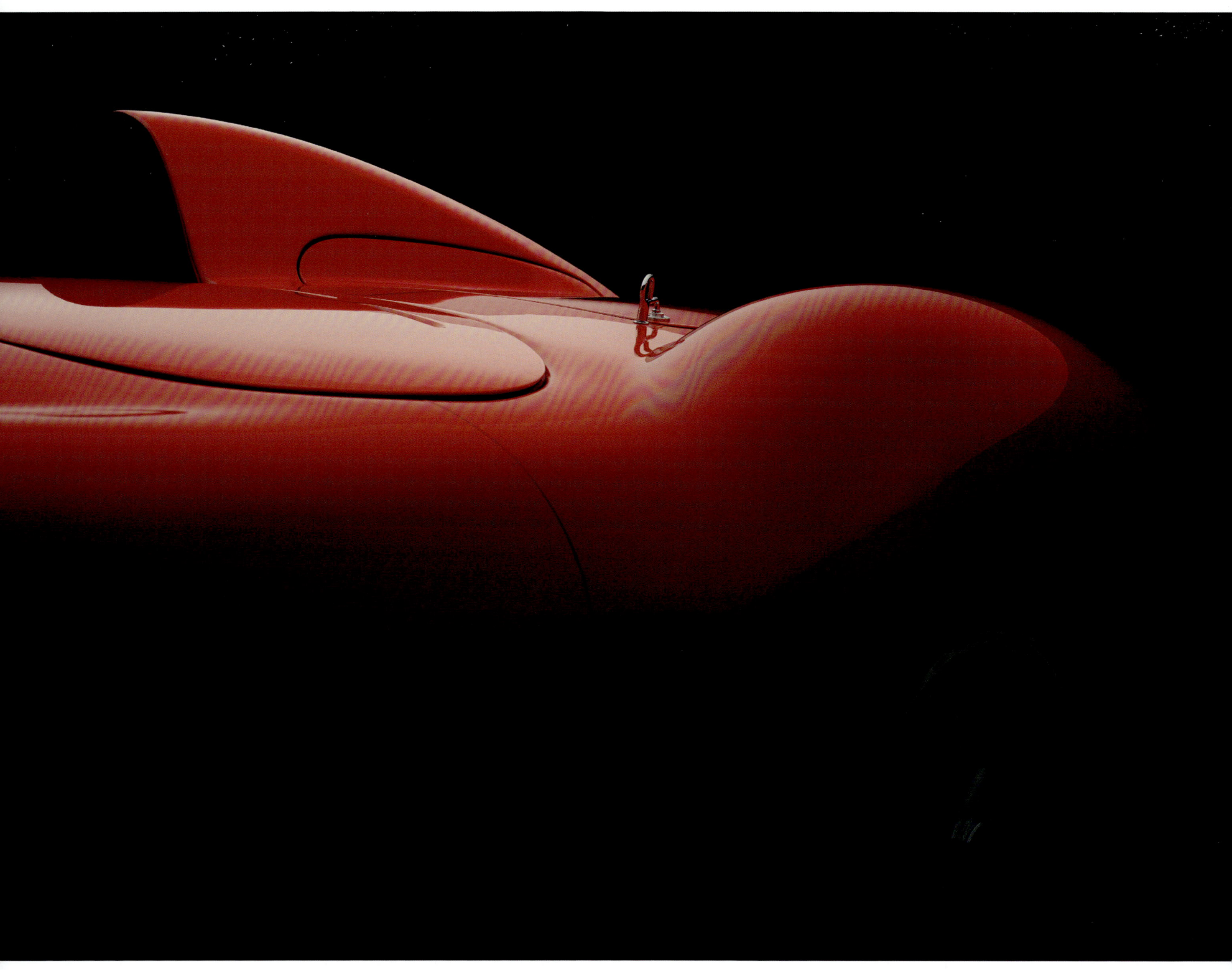

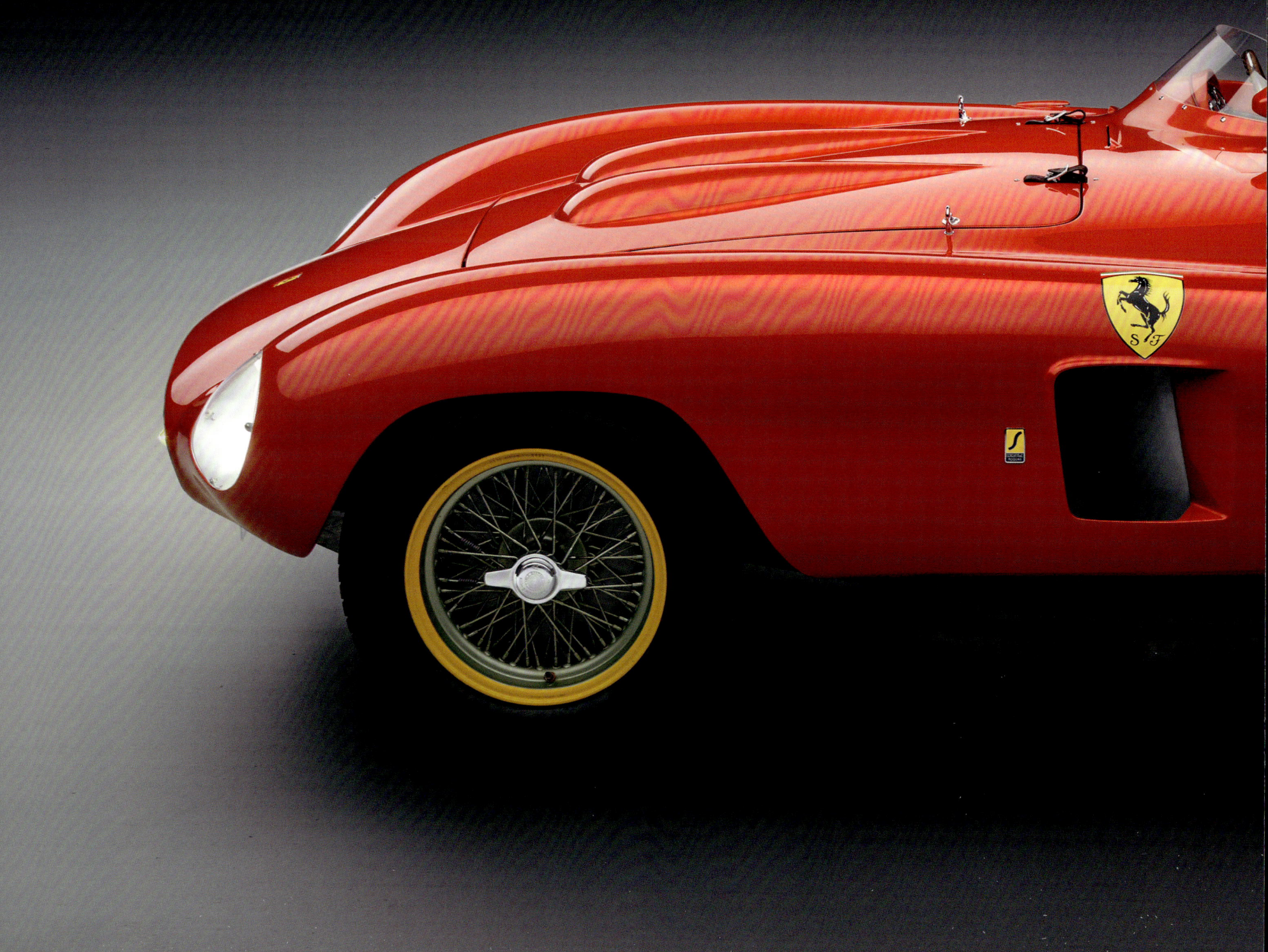

● The cockpit is Spartan in an elegant and traditional way, from its wood-rimmed steering wheel to its pair of textile-covered buckets seats that show sports racing cars were still designed to carry passengers in the mid-1950s.

● Even the gear lever has the appearance of an elegant sculpture. Modifications to the gear ratios have made a vast improvement to the driveability of the car on such as the modern Mille Miglia.

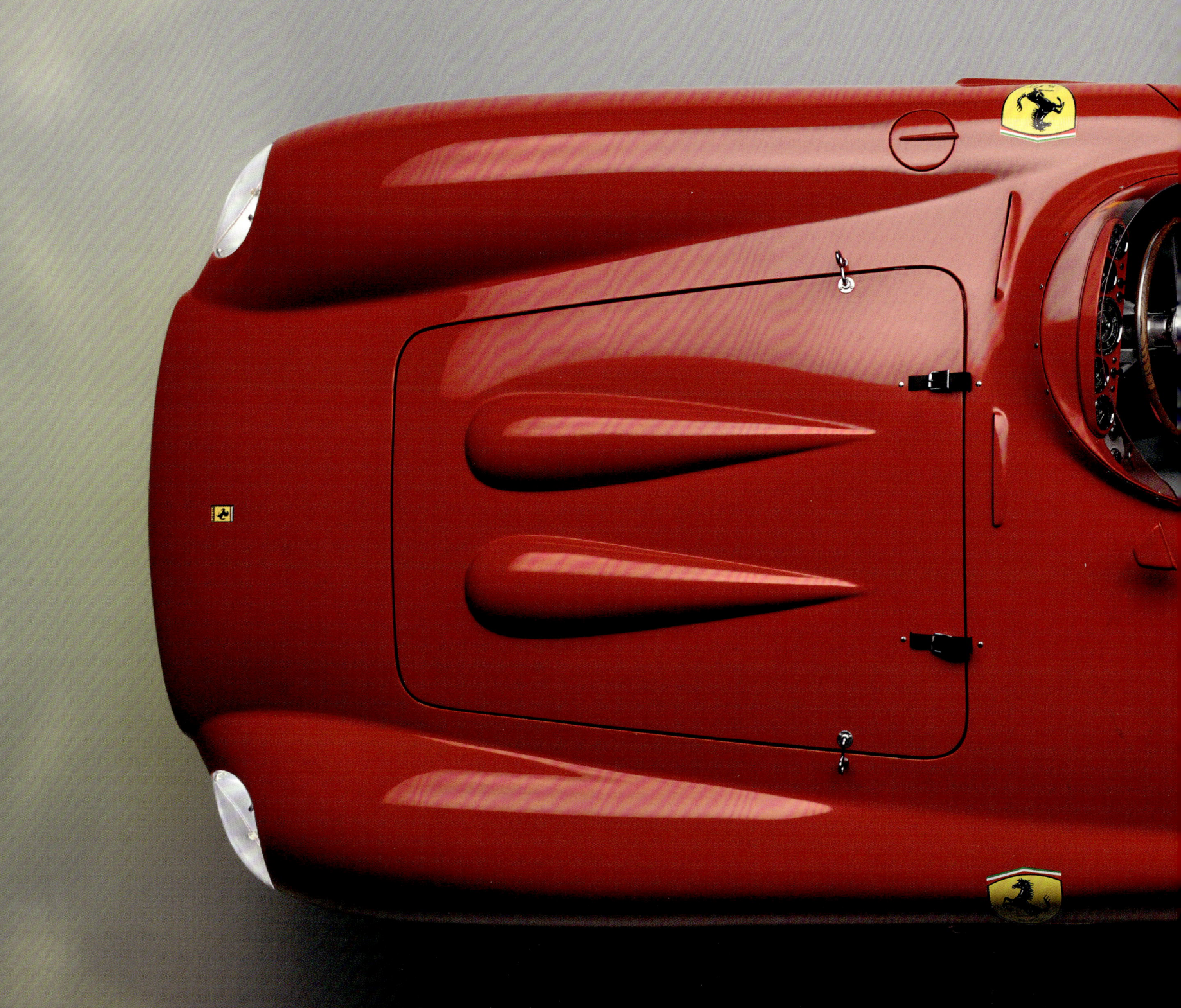

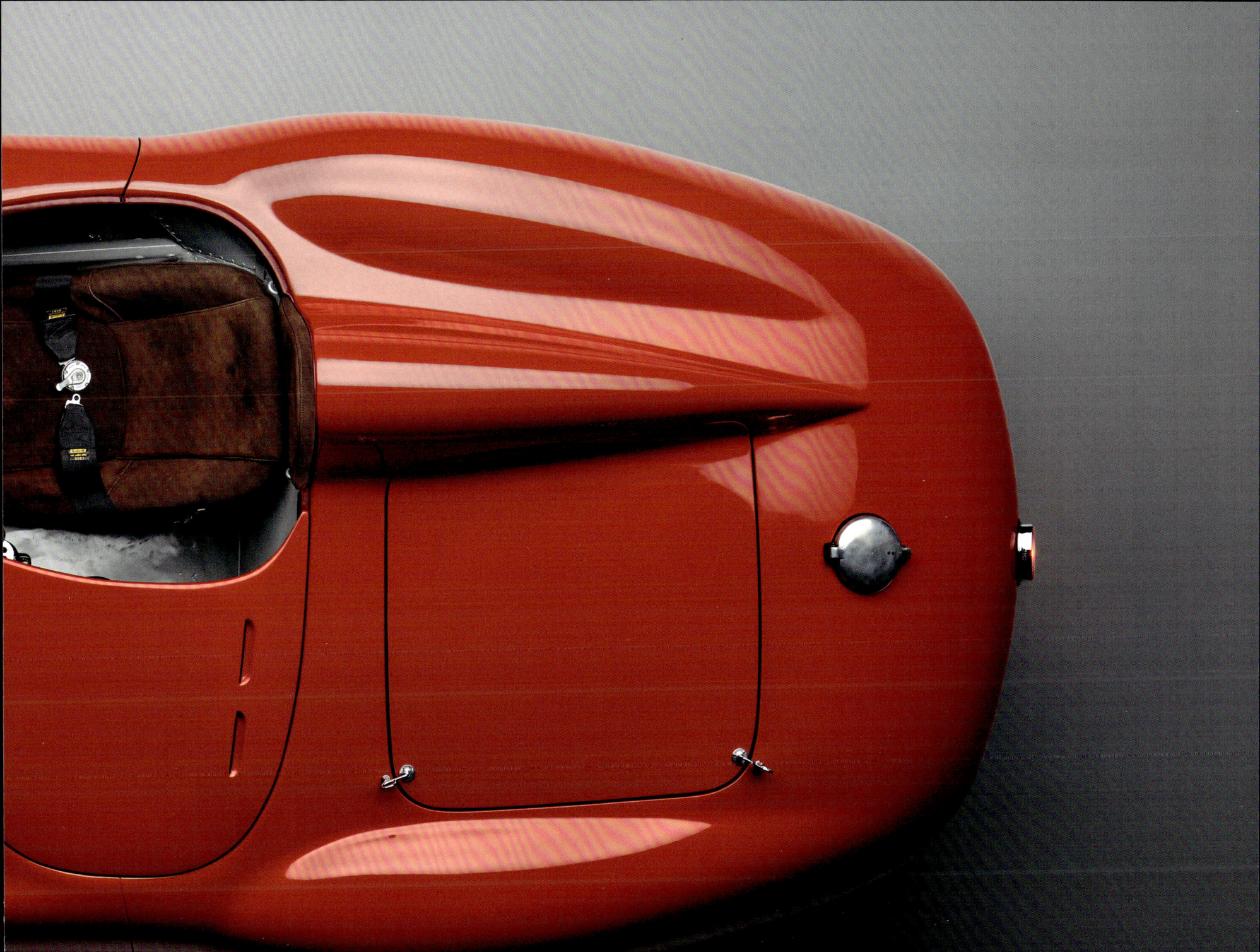

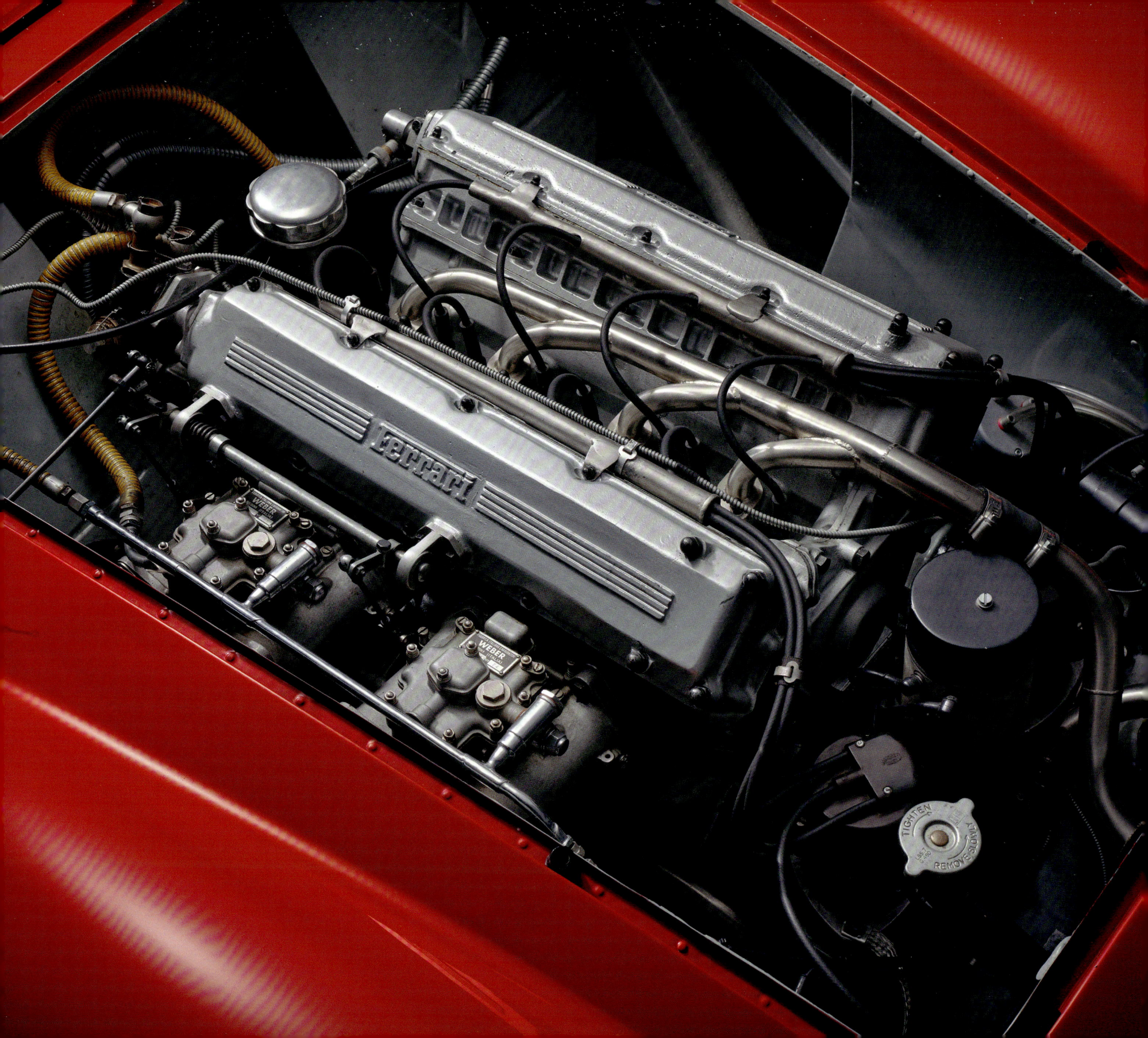

● Any possible confusion over the car's identity was shed once an obviously unoriginal, welded chassis plate had been removed. Underneath was a stamping that proved the car was, indeed, 0578M.

Drum brakes were still the order of the day at Ferrari in 1955. The independent suspension at the front featured unequal length wishbones, coil springs, hydraulic shock absorbers and an anti-roll bar, while a de Dion tube, twin radius arms, upper transverse leaf springs and hydraulic shock absorbers made up the rear suspension.

Exceptional Cars

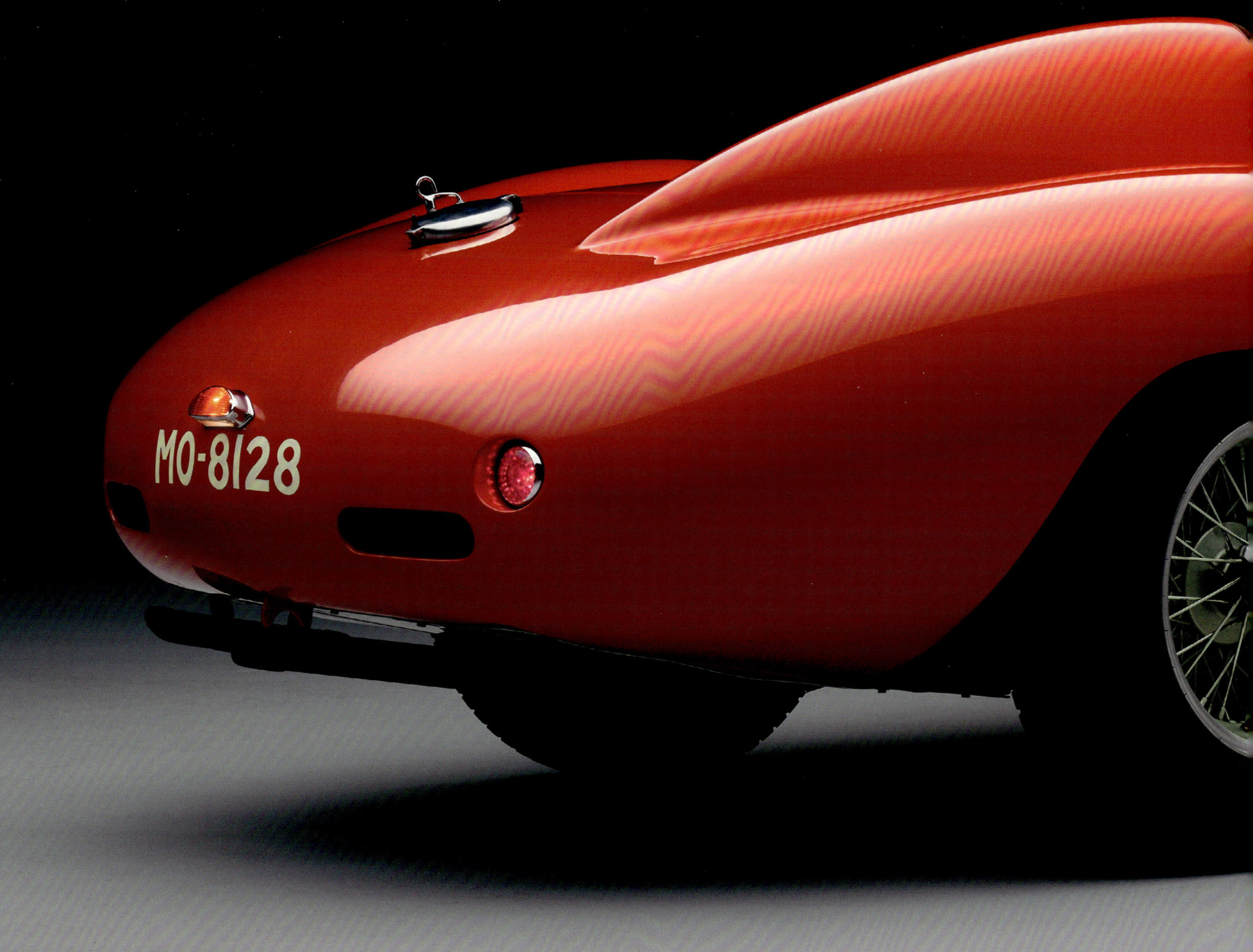

Acknowledgements

Kathy Ager, Cristián Bertschi, Andy Brown, Ben Dunnell, Dean Case, Andrew Cotton, Toby Crowe, Hasse Dahlriksson, Maria Dickson, Graham Earl, William Edgar, David Freestone, Howden Ganley, Graham Gauld, the Late Ken Gregory, Tony Griffiths, Rick Hall, Mark Holman, Alex Howe, Guillermo Iacona, Esa Illoinen, Terry Marshall, Cesare Martinengo, Doug Nye, Adolfo Orsi, Gary Pearson, Antoine Prunet, Tony Ring, Tony Robinson, Peter Sachs, Zoe Schafer, Martin Spetz, Diana and Matt Spitzley, Gill Wagstaff, Janos Wimpffen.

Bibliography

Allesandro and Massimo Acerbi *L'Aosta-Gran San Bernardo 1920/1957* Tipograffe La Vallée 1984
Piero Casucci *Enzo Ferrari 50 Years of Greatness* Haynes Publishing 1982
Gioachini Colombo *Origins of the Ferrari Legend* Haynes Publishing 1985
William Court *Grand Prix Requiem* PSL 1992
Cesare de Agostini *Castellotti A Stolen Heart* Giorgio Nada Editore 1984
Godfrey Eaton *Ferrari. The Road and Racing Cars* Haynes Publishing 1982
Enzo Ferrari *The Enzo Ferrari Memoires. My Terrible Joys* Hamish Hamilton 1963
Antonio Ghiai and others *Ferrari 1947-1997* Giorgio Nada Editore 1997
Mike Hawthorn *Challenge Me The Race* William Kimber 1958
Peter Higham *World Encyclopaedia of Racing Drivers* Haynes Publishing 2013
Richard Hough *Tourist Trophy* Hutchinson 1957
Karl Luvigsen *Italian Racing Red* Ian Allan 2008
Michael Lynch, William Edgar and Ron Parravano *American Sports Car Racing in the 1950s* Motorbooks 1998
Pete Lyons *Ferrari The Machines and The Man* Haynes Publishing 1989
Peter Miller *Conte Maggi's Mille Miglia* Alan Sutton 1988
Sir Stirling Moss with Alan Henry *All My Races* Haynes Publishing 2009
Sir Stirling Moss with Philip Porter *Stirling Moss Scrapbook 1955* Porter Press International 2005
Sir Stirling Moss with Philip Porter *Stirling Moss Scrapbook 1956-1960* Porter Press International 2009
Chris Nixon *Mon Ami Mate* Transport Bookman Publications 1991
David Owen *Targa Florio, Seventy Epic Years of Motor Racing* Haynes Publishing 1979
Paul Parker *Sports Car Racing in Camera 1950-59* Haynes Publishing 2010
Cyril Posthumus *World Sports Car Championship* MacGibbon & Kee 1961
Antoine Prunet *Ferrari Sports Racing and Prototype Competition Cars* Haynes Publishing 1983
Gino Rancati *Enzo Ferrari The Man* Haynes Publishing 1988
Hans Tanner with Doug Nye *Ferrari* Haynes Publishing 1979
John Starkey, Christope Renwick & Philippe Olczyk *Ferrari Fifty Years on the Track* Renwick and Starkey 1998
Graham Vercoe *The Golden Age of New Zealand Motor Racing* Reed Books 1993
Alec Ulmann *The Sebring Story* Chilton Book 1969
Ian Wagstaff *Maserati 250F Owners' Workshop Manual* Haynes Publishing 2014
János Wimpffen *Time and Two Seats* Motorsport Research Group 1999
Brock Yates *Enzo Ferrari The Man and the Machine* Doubleday 1991
Eoin Young *The Amazing Summer of '55* Haynes Publishing 2005
Various *Mille Miglia: The Ferrari and Mercedes Years* Brooklands Books 1996
Various *Targa Florio: Porsche and Ferrari Years, 1955-64* Brooklands Books 1999

Publications
Automobile Review
Autocar
Autocourse
Autosport
The Christchurch Star-Sun
Classic Cars
Motor Racing
Motor Sport
The Press (NZ)
Road & Track
Wheels

Index

Alfa Romeo (company) 10, 24
Alfa Romeo (car) 15, 73, 85
Allard J2 Cadillac 54
Armagnac, Paul 14
Ascari, Alberto 10, 12, 14, 15, 20, 23, 36, 47, 51, 90
Aston Martin DB3S 43, 59
Austin Healey
    100 35
    100M 63
    100S 69, 70, 73, 74, 75, 76, 79
Australian Tourist Trophy 70, 73
Autosport 32, 35, 41, 47, 48, 54, 57, 78, 84
Bazzi, Luigi 15
Behra, Jean 20, 23, 40, 41, 51, 54, 59, 70
Bellander, Björn 84, 88
Bellantani, Vittorio 15
Bellucci, Luigi 24, 25, 48
Berry, Bob 32
Bertilsson, Rune 80
Bjurström, Tore 80, 85
Bollaert, Lucio 54
Bolzano-Mendola hillclimb 27
Bonnier, Joakim 62, 76, 80, 82, 83, 85, 87
Bordoni, Franco 43
Brabham, Jack 29, 77, 78, 79, 80, 82, 83
Bremer, Carl-Otto 80
Bruno, Carlos 54
Bruno, Franco 54
Bueb, Ivor 26, 43
Buenos Aires 1000km 7, 26, 29, 31, 51, 52, 54, 57, 59, 62, 63
Busso, Giuseppe 15
Cabianca, Giulio 23, 24, 27, 48
Cahier, Bernard 44, 50
Carini, Piero 47, 48

Carlsson, Erik 80
Carlsson, Gunnar 85
Castellotti, Eugenio 17, 19, 20, 27, 28, 29, 32, 34, 35, 28, 39, 41, 43, 44, 47, 48, 51, 52, 58, 59, 60, 73, 90, 98
Chinetti, Luigi 31, 60, 66
Circuito del Mugello 23, 24
Clark, Tom 79
Collins, Peter 17, 47, 48, 51, 52, 60, 62, 88
Colombo, Gioacchino 10, 12, 15
Cooper-Climax 40, 77, 78
    T39 38, 43
    T49 80, 83, 87
Coppa D'Oro Delle Dolomiti 27
Cortese, Franco 18
Cumberland SCCA meeting 66
Daigh, Chuck 62
Dieci Ore Notturna Messinese 29
Dunedin Road Race, Dunedin 78, 79
Earl, Graham 88
Edgar, John 66
Eläintarhanajo, Helsinki 80, 85
Elford, Vic 36, 37
England, 'Lofty' 35
Ensley, Jack 59
Fangio, Juan Manuel 17, 19, 26, 43, 48, 51, 52, 54, 58, 59, 60, 73, 85
Farina, Nino 26, 36
Favera, Dalla 24
Ferrari (company) 7, 8, 10, 12, 13, 14, 15, 16, 17, 20, 23, 25, 26, 27, 28, 29, 32, 34, 35, 36, 37, 38, 40, 41, 44, 47, 48, 51, 52, 54, 57, 58, 60, 61, 62, 66, 67, 70, 73, 78, 80, 84, 85, 88, 90, 92, 96, 120
Ferrari (car) 8, 10, 12, 14, 15, 17, 18, 24, 29, 32, 36, 38, 39, 40, 41, 44, 47, 48, 51, 52, 54, 55, 57, 58, 59, 62, 67, 69, 70, 73, 74, 75, 79, 82, 85, 88, 90, 95, 98, 101

118 LM 31, 37, 92
121LM 67
125 10, 12, 70, 73
166MM 29
225S 54
250 Europa 47
250TR 29
290MM 51
335S 61
375 74
500 10, 47, 54, 59
500 Mondial 24, 47, 54, 59, 95
735S 10, 12
750 Monza 13, 20, 31, 32, 35, 47, 70, 79, 80, 85, 101
    857S 7, 16, 17, 28, 29, 32, 35, 38, 43, 48, 54, 58, 59, 65, 66, 69, 74, 80, 83, 88, 92, 95, 98, 101, 104
860 Monza 19, 59
Tipo 111 12, 16
Tipo 119 12, 16, 28, 38, 70
Tipo 129 15, 16, 52, 59, 70, 88
Tipo 500 15
Tipo 510 12, 15, 16
Tipo 555 12
Ferrari, Enzo 10, 12, 16, 23, 27, 28, 29, 36, 51, 61, 66, 67, 85
Filippis, Maria Teresa de 48
Fitch, John 35, 41, 43, 47, 48, 59
Fowler, Rob 95
Frachetti, Andrea 15
Frère, Paul 29
Gendebien, Olivier 27, 28, 29, 35, 52, 54, 57, 62, 63
Giardini, Francesco 48
Gibbons, Bob 74, 75
Ginther, Richie 62
Goldschmidt, Erwin 36

Gomez-Mena, Alfonso 59
Gonzáles, José Froilán 16, 31, 40, 47, 54
Gonzáles, Santiago 59
Gould, Horace 78, 79
Grand Prix 7, 13, 14, 29, 36, 40, 51, 62, 73, 75, 76, 77, 80, 85
    Australian 70, 76
    Belgian 51, 83
    Copenhagen 82
    Cuban 19
    French 26, 47
    Italian 90,
    Monaco 29, 34, 51
    New Zealand 69, 70, 73, 74, 75, 76, 77
    Sebring 66
    Senigallia 10
    Supercortemaggiore, Monza 15, 20, 23, 26, 35
    Swedish 17, 62, 80, 85
Grant, Gregor 47, 48
Gregory, Ken 77
Gregory, Masten 35, 38, 43, 51, 58, 59
Gurney, Dan 62
Hall, Rick 92, 95, 96
Hamilton, Duncan 17
Hansgen, Walt 59
Hanstein, Huschke von 36
Harris, Ken 18, 79
Haskell, Isabell 54
Hawthorn, Mike 10, 13, 14, 16, 17, 20, 23, 26, 32, 38, 41, 59
Herrmann, Hans 59
Hill, Graham 29
Hill, Phil 26, 29, 36, 52, 54, 57, 58, 59, 62, 63, 85
Imola, Coppa Shell 24, 25
Jaguar (company) 20, 26, 44, 58

Jaguar (car)
    C-type 29, 73
    D-type 26, 59, 70, 73
    XK120 69, 74
Jano, Vittorio 15
Jansson, Ake 84
Jaras, Raul 54
Jenkinson, Denis 44, 77, 90
Jensen, Ross 18, 69, 70, 73, 74, 75, 76-77, 78, 79
Jensen, Syd 74, 75
Kanonloppet, Karlskoga 80, 82, 83, 84, 85, 87
Karlsson, Tom 80
Keele, Mike 83
Kimberly, Jim 58, 59, 60, 65, 67
Klemantaski, Louis 17
Kling, Karl 43, 48
Kovacs-Jones, Eduardo 54
Kvanström, John 17, 80, 82, 83, 85, 87
L'Aosta-Gran San Bernardo hillclimb 28
Lady Wigram Trophy 69, 70, 73, 75, 78
Lampredi, Aurelio 10, 12, 15, 16
Laurea, Gérard 14
Le Mans 24, 26, 27, 28, 29, 31, 32, 34, 35, 36, 38, 40, 42, 43, 44, 52, 54, 62, 66, 70, 73
Levegh, Pierre 32, 34, 35
Lincoln, Curt 83, 87
Lippi, Osbvaldo 48
Lister, Brian 77
Lister-Jaguar 75, 76, 80
Ljungfeldt, Bo 83
Lostalo, Carlos 54
Louwman, Evert 88
Lovely, Pete 59
Lucas, Jean 35
Lundgren, Erik 17, 85

MacDowel, Michael 43
Macklin, Lance 35, 43
Maglioli, Umberto 10, 12, 16, 17, 20, 23, 24, 25, 28, 29, 32, 34, 35, 36, 37, 38, 41, 43, 44, 47, 48, 52, 62, 90, 92, 98
Mainwaring, Richard 41
Maiocchi, Angel 54
Manzon, Robert 44, 47, 48
Margulies, Dan 29, 88
Marzotto, Paolo 90
Marzotto, Vittorio 13, 14,
Maserati (company) 10, 15, 77
Maserati (car) 20, 28, 52, 54, 77
    150S 54
    200S 83, 87
    250F 51, 62, 73, 74, 75, 76, 77, 78, 79
    300S 43, 52, 54, 59, 70
    8CLT 79
    A6GCS 24, 25, 27, 48
    Tipo 61 83, 84
Massimino, Alberto 15
Mayers, Jim 38
McAfee, Jack 36, 59, 66
McKinney, David 79
McLaren, Bruce 76, 77
McMillan, John 79
Menditéguy, Carlos 52, 54
Mercedes-Benz (company) 14, 16, 17, 26, 27, 28, 32, 34, 36, 38, 41, 44, 47, 48, 51, 52, 77
Mercedes-Benz (car)
    300SL 26, 27
    300SLR 15, 26, 29, 32, 35, 43, 47, 48, 51, 54, 85
Mille Miglia 7, 13, 14, 17, 18, 27, 31, 32, 36, 37, 47, 51, 61, 90, 92, 95, 96, 98, 101, 110
Monk, June 79
Moores, Nigel 88

Moss, Stirling 26, 32, 35, 37, 38, 40, 41, 43, 47, 48, 51, 52, 54, 62, 70, 73, 74, 76, 77, 80, 82, 83, 85, 87, 90
Motor Sport 44
Muro, Enrique 54
Musso, Giuseppe 48
Musso, Luigi 17, 20, 23, 43, 47, 51, 52, 58, 59, 62, 66
Naylor, Brian 88
Nelson, Ed 61
Neubauer, Alfred 44
New Zealand Championship Road Race, Ryal Bush 79
Nürburgring 1000km 17, 19, 29, 32, 44, 62
Osca MT4 1500 48
Parkes, Mike 37
Parnell, Reg 43, 70, 74, 75, 76, 78, 79
Pauley, Jim 59
Pearson, Gary 96, 98
Perdisa, Cesare 24, 25, 59
Persson, Olle 80
Pilette, Andre 80
Piper, David 83, 84
Pira, Salvatore La 48
Pitt, Bill 70
Pola, Julio 54
Poore, Dennis 43
Porsche (company) 35, 37, 58, 81
Porsche (car)
    550 Spyder 43, 59, 66
Portago, Alfonso de 17, 19, 58, 59, 60, 61, 65, 67, 85
Posthumus, Cyril 13, 14, 36
Prunet, Antoine 15, 16, 27, 70, 79, 80, 88, 92
RAC Tourist Trophy, Dundrod 7, 13, 16, 32, 34, 35, 43
Road & Track 37, 44, 50, 84
Robinson, Tony 29
Rossi, Giuseppe 48
Roycroft, Roy 74, 78, 79

Rubirosa, Porfirio 59
Salvadori, Roy 43, 59
Sanderson, Ninian 32
Scaglietti, Sergio 16, 104
Scarlatti, Giorgio 48
Schell, Harry 24, 25, 31, 58, 59
Scott Brown, Archie 77
Scuderia Ferrari 24, 26, 36, 44, 47, 80, 85
Sebring 12-Hours 7, 8, 26, 29, 31, 32, 37, 51, 52, 58, 59, 62, 67
Shelby, Carroll 43, 59, 62, 66
Shuter, Frank 79
Sighinolfi, Sergio 44, 47, 48, 90
Simon, André 43
Smith, Bill 38
South Island Championship Road Race, Mairehau 79
Spence, Mike 62
Spencer-Nairn, Angus 88, 95
Starrabba, Gaetano 48
Stilwell, Bib 70
Stringer, Alex 74
Swaters, Jacques 41
Sweikert, Bob 59
Tanner, Hans 10
Targa Florio 7, 29, 36, 37, 44, 47, 48, 50
Taruffi, Piero 10, 25, 31, 35, 38, 41, 43, 44, 59, 90
Titterington, Desmond 38, 41, 47, 48
Tomasi, Carlo 54
Tomaso, Alejandro de 54
Trintignant, Maurice 13, 16, 26, 29, 31, 34, 35, 38, 40, 41, 42, 43, 62, 85
Trips, Wolfgang von 43, 59
Valenzano, Gino 27
Valenzano, Piero 27
Villoresi, Luigi 12, 47, 51

Walker, Peter 43
Walker, Rob 26, 40
Walters, Phil 26
Wharton, Ken 18, 70, 73, 74, 75, 79
Whitehead, Graham 35, 38, 73, 83
Whitehead, Peter 35, 38, 41, 69, 70, 73, 74, 75, 76, 78, 79, 80, 83, 88
World Sportscar Championship 8, 32, 36, 43, 44, 48, 80, 85, 88
Young, Eoin 73, 79
Zeuner, Wolf 88